"For anyone feeling the ever-present invitation to embrace cynicism as reality, doomscrolling as a daily habit, and isolation as a form of protection from getting your heart broken—this book will help you take a fragment of optimism and transform it into an unshakable hope."

Eric Brown, co-founder and chief vision officer, Whiteboard

"While inspiring, *The Gift of Disillusionment* is also spine-straightening and convicting, cutting to the heart of the reader to strip away all delusions of self-sufficiency we are so prone to, in order to place God in His rightful place at the center of our leadership. This is an exceptionally relevant guide on how to embody long-lasting, godly leadership and effectively persevere in God's calling. This is a must-read for any Christian seeking to sustainably pursue God's call in their life."

Michael Lindsay, president, Taylor University;
author of *Hinge Moments*

"*The Gift of Disillusionment* is a much-needed reminder to the body of Christ that true, enduring hope is fulfilled through our reliance on God and commitment to redemptive work. Peter Greer and Chris Horst masterfully weave Scripture with stories of exemplary servant leaders to illustrate the promise of God: that we will all experience challenges, loss, and pain, but He walks alongside us every step of the way. For those who are similarly called and committed to stepping into spaces of brokenness, this book presents principles to help press beyond cynicism and fatigue into a position of humble surrender, anchored by the knowledge that eternal hope rests solely in the goodness of God."

Vivian Long, executive director, Long Family Foundation

"Greer and Horst deliver just the wisdom and restorative insight we need in our tumultuous times. *The Gift of Disillusionment* is rich with healing and hopeful perspective, not the thin hope of marketing brochures but the rooted and persevering hope of Jeremiah 17. After a decade of reading and writing on hope, I nearly wept at the profound importance of this work."

Scott Todd, president, One Child

"Peter and Chris's encouraging new book gathers a poignant collection of stories about serious challenges to faith. They view them through the lens of the paradoxical blessing of disillusionment. Highlighting this theme, they remind us of an important truth: Christian works promoting justice and charity point to a new age but do not bring it about. Instead, we are left with the humility of the moment as a sign-post; we are, as James says, blessed in the doing, not because of it. Yet that is the source of our energy and where our focus always should be. This blessing is essentially the same as that of the transformed world for which we long: communion with the Triune One, joy of all ages."

Douglas R. Forrester, chair, Rising Tide Capital

"From the opening declaration of *The Gift of Disillusionment*, through the book's final proclamation to look upward toward Christ, authors Peter Greer and Chris Horst provide a compelling case for the long view of Christ-centered leadership—sustaining a lifetime of faithful service to God despite the inevitable challenges and disappointments encountered along the journey. The narrative testimonies of biblical, historical, and contemporary leaders included in the volume provide a rich tapestry of wisdom, insights, and practical suggestions for nurturing hope even in the most difficult of circumstances. I look forward to sharing this remarkable book with the members of my leadership team."

Kim Phipps, president, Messiah University

"In my thirty-year career of working among the urban poor, I've seen too many people with idealistic, good intentions to change the world get weary in well doing and sometimes even leave the faith. This book provides a blueprint to see our challenges realistically and gives us a roadmap concerning how to not lose our faith as we do the work of the ministry."

Alvin Sanders, president and CEO, World Impact

"Grounded in Scripture and stories from around the globe, *The Gift of Disillusionment* is a must-read for all of us longing for hope in a world full of disappointments. It addresses the question of our day, 'How do we hold on to hope—hope that endures?'"

Tom Lin, president and CEO, InterVarsity Christian Fellowship

"All of us who have led purpose-driven organizations have felt the challenges, discouragement, and personal sacrifices that accompany trying to change the status quo. At various moments in the journey of leading change, we are inevitably faced with the question, 'Is it worth it?' It is at these moments that the stories and encouragement of this book are most helpful. This book challenges leaders to look upward rather than inward during discouraging times to find our true hope."

Mike Bontrager, founder and retired CEO, Chatham Financial;
founder and president, Square Root Collective

"Through the stories and Scriptures interwoven in *The Gift of Disillusionment*, Peter and Chris remind all of us who have a heart for ministry and service that our idealism will undoubtedly be met with the realities of living in a fallen world. These realities will barrage us with waves that not only challenge our missional resolve but test the very vitality of our faith. Yet, despite the cynicism, heartache, pain, and discouragement, Peter and Chris challenge us to forge ahead because God is at work! And more times than not, His greatest work is by way of the blood, sweat, tears—and yes, faith—of those who break through the barrier of disillusionment by turning upward instead of inward, because 'He who began [this] good work will be faithful to bring it to completion!'"

Chilobe Kalambo, managing member, Kalambo Consulting

"Any leader facing the enormous challenges that come after idealism fades should read Peter and Chris's book. It offers practical, real-life stories of leaders in unimaginable circumstances who do not wallow in the cynicism of today's culture but sustain long-term service with optimism and hope. Their stories and scriptural foundation inspire me to lead differently—and in doing so, demonstrate a sustainable hope only found by faith in God."

Lisa Payne, retired chief financial officer and chief
administrative officer, Taubman Centers, Inc.

"In *The Gift of Disillusionment*, Peter and Chris offer language for what philanthropists and nonprofit leaders know to be true: This is really hard. The complicated and messy dynamics facing givers and ministries rarely make great stories in annual reports, but they are our shared reality."

Josh Kwan, president, The Gathering

"If you have ever felt discouraged because the hopes you had for the future were dashed by the present-day reality of your life, this book is for you. Peter and Chris act as skilled guides, showing us how to hold on to hope by turning our gaze upward when everything in us wants to turn inward. Prepare to be reminded that we can dare to hope, no matter what setbacks we may face. This book will show you how!"

Jason Mitchell, teaching pastor, LCBC Church;
author of *No Easy Jesus*

"This wise and beautiful book draws on insights from Christ-followers with decades in the trenches of a mystery: the strange place where we know it's *God's* job to save the world, and yet *we* are called to be His instruments. Greer and Horst reveal how this is the place where the gift of disillusionment awaits; the gift that strips away self-confidence and pivots our gaze upward so we can find the courage to keep moving forward. I was deeply encouraged by these saints' steadfast reliance on King Jesus and the persevering joy that emerged from that. Highly recommended for all those needing a fresh injection of realistic, informed, God-centered hope that can shrink the shadows cast by brokenness and suffering."

Amy L. Sherman, author of *Agents of Flourishing:*
Pursuing Shalom in Every Corner of Society

THE GIFT OF
DISILLUSIONMENT

Books by Peter Greer and Chris Horst

The Gift of Disillusionment (with Brianna Lapp and Jill Heisey)

Rooting for Rivals (with Jill Heisey)

Entrepreneurship for Human Flourishing

Mission Drift (with Anna Haggard)

Books by Peter Greer

Succession (coauthored by Doug Fagerstrom with Brianna Lapp)

The Redemptive Nonprofit (coauthored by Jena Lee Nardella and Praxis)

The Board and the CEO (coauthored by David Weekley)

Created to Flourish (coauthored by Phil Smith)

The Giver and the Gift (coauthored by David Weekley)

40/40 Vision (coauthored by Greg Lafferty)

Watching Seeds Grow (coauthored by Keith Greer)

The Spiritual Danger of Doing Good (with Anna Haggard)

Mommy's Heart Went Pop! (coauthored by Christina Kyllonen)

The Poor Will Be Glad (coauthored by Phil Smith)

THE GIFT OF DISILLUSIONMENT

ENDURING **HOPE** FOR LEADERS AFTER IDEALISM FADES

PETER GREER AND **CHRIS HORST**

BETHANYHOUSE
a division of Baker Publishing Group
Minneapolis, Minnesota

Published by Bethany House Publishers
11400 Hampshire Avenue South
Minneapolis, Minnesota 55438
www.bethanyhouse.com

Bethany House Publishers is a division of
Baker Publishing Group, Grand Rapids, Michigan

Printed in the United States of America

Library of Congress Cataloging-in-Publication Data
Names: Greer, Peter, author. | Horst, Chris, author.
Title: The gift of disillusionment : enduring hope for leaders after idealism fades / Peter Greer and Chris Horst.
Description: Minneapolis, Minnesota : Bethany House Publishers, a division of Baker Publishing Group, [2022] | Includes bibliographical references.
Identifiers: LCCN 2021046297 | ISBN 9780764238260 (cloth)
Subjects: LCSH: Hope—Religious aspects—Christianity. | Expectation (Psychology)—Religious aspects—Christianity. | Cynicism. | Idealism. | Resilience (Personality trait)—Religious aspects—Christianity.
Classification: LCC BV4638 .G725 2022 | DDC 234/.25—dc23
LC record available at https://lccn.loc.gov/2021046297

Unless otherwise indicated, Scripture quotations are taken from the Holy Bible, New Living Translation, copyright © 1996, 2004, 2015 by Tyndale House Foundation. Used by permission of Tyndale House Publishers, Inc., Carol Stream, Illinois 60188. All rights reserved.

Scripture quotations labeled ESV are from The Holy Bible, English Standard Version® (ESV®), copyright © 2001 by Crossway, a publishing ministry of Good News Publishers. Used by permission. All rights reserved. ESV Text Edition: 2016

Scripture quotations labeled MSG are taken from THE MESSAGE, copyright © 1993, 2002, 2018 by Eugene H. Peterson. Used by permission of NavPress. All rights reserved. Represented by Tyndale House Publishers, Inc.

Scripture quotations labeled NIV are from THE HOLY BIBLE, NEW INTERNATIONAL VERSION®, NIV® Copyright © 1973, 1978, 1984, 2011 by Biblica, Inc.® Used by permission. All rights reserved worldwide.

Scripture quotations labeled NKJV are from the New King James Version®. Copyright © 1982 by Thomas Nelson. Used by permission. All rights reserved.

Cover design by LOOK Design Studio
Journey illustrations by Jeff Brown

Authors are represented by Wolgemuth and Associates.

Baker Publishing Group publications use paper produced from sustainable forestry practices and post-consumer waste whenever possible.

22 23 24 25 26 27 28   7 6 5 4 3 2 1

Dedicated to London and Mack.

You fill us with hope.

CONTENTS

Contents

CHAPTER 1
INVITATION TO HOPE

Please make the bad news stop.

For most of our lives, we've been committed—even passionate—followers of the news and global events. We have valued information as the foundation for involvement. But in the last season—when racial injustice, political polarization, and the moral failures of prominent leaders dominated the headlines—we've felt that knowledge drive us not to engagement but to discouragement.

Bad news surrounds us, and it feels as though the frequency and volume of these stories are increasing.

If the headlines tell the whole story, then our world has every reason to lose hope.

As followers of Jesus, it's particularly painful when we read of people within the faith community whose words and actions betray our faith. Who claim to follow Jesus but use power and position to subjugate, not serve. Duplicity and hypocrisy, #MeToo and #ChurchToo movements, and viciousness from people who pin crosses on their blazers.

In the wake of all this bad news in the world and in our churches, we talked with friends whose faith was faltering. We witnessed the fallout of elevating leaders to a godlike status, only to watch their very human flaws undermine their credibility and leave a trail of destruction—and often a crisis of faith—behind.

At the height of our own discouragement, we uncovered a story about early believers in AD 260. During a deadly plague that inspired a frenzied mass exodus from Athens, Christians rushed into the infected city to care for the sick and dying whom others had left behind. Dionysius, the first bishop of Athens, noted believers' remarkable willingness to rush toward the dying at the risk of losing their own lives. He commended them for their "unbounded love and loyalty," their pattern of "never sparing themselves and thinking only of one another. Heedless of danger, they took charge of the sick, attending to their every need and ministering to them in Christ."[1] They put their faith into action through self-sacrifice, and the world was turned upside down.

Does faith in Christ still have the power to prompt sacrificial, world-changing action? Can it still motivate people to battle disease, fight injustice, and alleviate poverty—not just for days or weeks but faithfully for a lifetime? Can it transform our self-centered hearts, making us people who don't just speak of the good news but live as though it's a reality?

We often hear about and retell inspiring stories of the way the Church showed up thousands of years ago. But we needed the assurance that these aren't just "early Church stories." That beyond the bad news that dominates the headlines, there is an incredible amount of *good news* in the world today.

To find it, we temporarily closed our newsfeeds and silenced the daily doses of discouraging stories. Jill and Brianna came alongside us to study the biblical virtue of hope as it's portrayed in the pages of Scripture. We also turned to the wisdom of trusted friends to point us to present-day accounts of the courageous faith, hope, and love of God's people transforming communities around the world.

Throughout our careers, we have served alongside, partnered with, and admired global leaders who routinely face corrupt governments, religious persecution, natural disasters, and extreme poverty. And while we have had countless conversations with men and women leading and serving in difficult circumstances, until researching this book, we had never overtly asked, "What keeps you there? What sustains your life of service? How have you not given in to discouragement? How do you hold on to hope?" It was time to start asking.

Longing for Hope

In society we see many monetizing and marketing their solutions to hopelessness and despair. Leadership gurus promise easy hacks to resolve our disappointments and deepest struggles. Instagram influencers outline diet and exercise plans guaranteeing a healthier life. Technology companies insist their latest app will decrease our stress and anxiety, bring peace to our relationship challenges, improve our sleep, and make us look younger.

In 2020, "self-care" expanded to a $450 billion industry, forty-five times larger than it was just one decade earlier.[2] From Fitbit to candles and from self-help books to meditation apps, we are spending close to half a trillion dollars annually in our attempt to find hope.

But our experience is that these solutions leave us utterly unsatisfied. Our Western cultural obsession with self-improvement is insufficient. Rates of depression, anxiety, stress, and suicidal thoughts continue to increase throughout the United States.[3] We are spending more time and money but coming up empty. More than half of Americans say they are more anxious today than they were one year ago.[4]

Within the Church, the solutions Christians propose are often equally unhelpful. Trite Jeremiah 29:11 memes assuring us our hardships are NBD ("no big deal") because God has a plan aren't helpful. "It will all work out" is not just untrue: It is hurtful. We don't need any more advice amounting to tying theological bows on hardship.

Cultural remedies point us to something we can discover or architect within ourselves: "Look within and find your inner strength." But the Old Testament prophets and the modern-day leaders we feature in this book describe a very different journey and conclusion: Within is the wrong place to look.

We cannot master our circumstances, engineer our happiness, or find refuge from real pain. We cannot avoid hardship and deep disappointment. We are unable to control all our circumstances.

When everything feels like it's falling apart, how do we respond? How do we find hope? Where do we turn to navigate the troubles we'll inevitably encounter in ourselves, in our organizations, and in our service?

The Guides

As we sought to understand what sustains a lifetime of faithful service, we asked our wisest peers, *Who are the pioneers responsible for leading organizations and demonstrating "long obedience in the same direction"?*[5]

We sought leaders with a minimum of twenty years of service in their fields and interviewed those who demonstrated staying power, sticking around long enough to experience the thorniest and knottiest difficulties. We intentionally sought leaders who had wounds and setbacks that could have forced them to give up—but who pressed on anyway.

In a world consumed with short-term results, quick fixes, and instant gratification, we wanted to uncover the beauty and strength of long-term commitment. We wanted to understand what builds and sustains leaders of hope and resilience.

We applaud people who serve four years. We admire people who serve forty.

Through in-person conversations or phone interviews, we spent time exploring the underlying beliefs, faith, and practices that sustain the long-term service of these global leaders.

From the streets of Guatemala City to the academy in Wrocław, Poland, from a school in Oklahoma City to a jail cell in Zimbabwe, we can't wait to introduce you to the leaders we met. These are not stories of sanitized saints or easy wins. They all faced unimaginable struggles and disappointments. They inspired, challenged, and taught us as we explored their stories of running toward need rather than from it, cultivating hopeful communities, and spurring lasting movements.

These stories are not of individual heroism but rather of a God who is present in pain and heartache—a God who doesn't seem to solve all the problems in the way we might like—yet is enough.[6] These leaders pointed us to the inspiration and truth they relied upon in Scripture. Again and again, they referenced Jeremiah, the curious Old Testament prophet who wrote the longest book in the Bible and is known as "The Weeping Prophet." The prophet and the eponymous book seemed like unlikely authorities on the virtue of *hope*, but Jeremiah inspired us, too, and provided the framework for this book.

Chapter 6 details Jeremiah's story. For now, suffice it to say that Jeremiah understood a thing or two about holding on to hope, even when the world fell apart all around him. He delivered God's truth to people who were lost in self-reliance, nationalism, and the worship of false gods. He continued speaking as the Jews lived as exiles and refugees, their once-enemies now their rulers. As their world came apart, Jeremiah reminded them, and reminds us, where hope can be found.

In a world bombarded with negative news, we need a biblical perspective on enduring hope and stories of courageous service in our world today. And we need the global Church. For too long, global and marginalized communities have been the recipients of international aid and charity, yet seldom are they recognized as teachers and mentors, those rich with wisdom and experience who have much to offer us. It's far past time to recognize our need to be taught by the witness of the Church beyond, as well as within, our borders. North to South, East to West, we need each other in this journey.

The End of Idealism

Serving in ten different countries across the globe, the group we profile is diverse—in geography, interests, background, gender, culture, and a host of other factors—but in their stories, a consistent pattern emerged. While we will emphasize a single attribute of each leader in the chapters to come, there were glaring similarities in their leadership journeys. Multiple times we listened with delight to the curious repetition of key phrases and ideas.

Almost always, these leaders described beginning their service full of **idealism,** brimming with hopes and dreams.

Idealists see a need and feel an inner prompt to respond. Not content to merely bemoan injustice or just ponder how to respond, they step out with the courage to *do something*.

Idealism is rooted in the recognition of what's wrong in the world and a longing to see it made right. It motivates leaders to take a stand for justice and fight for a cause. It's a desire to see God's "will be done on earth, as it is in heaven."[7] At its core, idealism is built on promise and possibility—a vision of what could be.

But sooner or later, our expectations collide with our experiences. We realize there is more complexity, nuance, and challenge than we anticipated. We learn it's harder to solve problems than we thought. People disappoint us. Teams run into conflict. There are no easy solutions to deeply entrenched problems.

Idealism is also besieged by the pain we experience. From poverty alleviation to racial justice to foster care to missions to education reform, service inflicts wounds. If we love others, we will inevitably experience hurt and disappointment. As lawyer and activist Bryan Stevenson says in his book *Just Mercy*, "You can't effectively fight abusive power, poverty, inequality, illness, oppression, or injustice and not be broken by it."[8]

Idealism and optimism draw us in, but they eventually feel incompatible with the complicated reality we experience. We nurse our wounds and wonder if it's really worth it. We learn how inadequate and incapable we are to do what we set out to do. Our idealism clashes with reality, leaving battle wounds on our hearts. Inevitably, we realize the insufficiency of our abilities and reach the end of our idealism.

Our unmet expectations and painful experiences lead to **disillusionment.**

Consulting firm McKinsey describes disillusionment as "occurring when deeply held beliefs and expectations are challenged by circumstances."[9] Shattered assumptions can shake even the most optimistic leaders.

Idealism lasts only if we bury our heads in the sand, willfully ignoring the complexity and depth of the problems we're addressing. When our expectations and experiences inevitably collide, disillusionment results. And it's unsettling.

As we began our research, we expected disillusionment to be a challenge leaders must endure and overcome. We've instead come to see it as a pivot point on every leader's journey.

Wrapped in the pain of disillusionment is a gift: It's an invitation to turn not inward but upward.

The Journey from Idealism to Enduring Hope

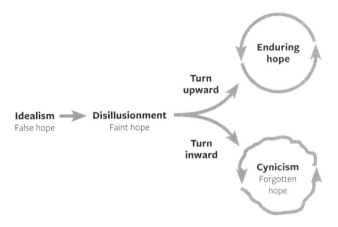

Turn Inward

If we turn inward, we follow the well-trod path to **cynicism**.

Comedian George Carlin once said, "If you scratch any cynic, you find a disappointed idealist."[10]

The cynic begins as an idealist but then resolves, *It just cannot be done. We're wasting our time. People don't change. It doesn't really matter. What God has called us to is impossible.*

Cynicism prompts us to slip back from the dance floor and move to a place of safe distance in the balcony, where we can smugly critique the moves of others. *Look at those ridiculous dance moves*, we criticize.[11]

Fearful of getting hurt, cynics build shells of self-protection and self-preservation. They abandon hope for themselves and mock it as naïveté in others. Cynics resign themselves to perpetual hopelessness.

Cynical leaders damage themselves and those around them. In conversations with enthusiastic people who want to engage in solving problems, such leaders regale them with bitter stories beginning with a knowing eye roll: *Let me tell you why you would never want to do that.*

Seeing only what is wrong with the world, cynicism acknowledges the pain of a post-Eden reality while denying the reality that God "has promised new creation."[12]

And cynicism is on the rise. When a recent poll asked Americans whom they most admired, the most common answer by far was "nobody."[13]

As the young composer Mohammed Fairouz summarizes, "The age of anxiety has given way to the age of cynicism. Among my generation, cynicism is no longer a bad word; it's being celebrated."[14]

When hope dims, cynicism lurks close behind. It's a contagion, spreading throughout our churches and organizations with blistering speed. It's seen every time someone gives in to the belief that the world is broken beyond repair or that individuals and institutions will never

Cynicism isn't neutral ground; it corrodes and corrupts.

get any better. We might still go through the motions, but we no longer believe that real progress is possible.

Around the world, Christian leaders and organizations see hope slipping away, both in themselves and in their organizations. Idealism does not sustain. Disappointment leads to disillusionment. The siren call of cynicism promises sanctuary to hurting hearts and wounded egos, but cynicism isn't neutral ground; it corrodes and corrupts.

The Invitation

This book expresses our longing to figure out how to move beyond the false hope of idealism, the faint hope of disillusionment, and the forgotten hope of cynicism. It is a journey to discover an enduring hope that enlivens and sustains our service. We want to figure out how to be, as the book of Jeremiah puts it, "serene and calm through droughts, bearing fresh fruit every season."[15]

We promise this book will point to *real* hope, not to happy endings. We will not minimize or rationalize the pain we all endure. We will not slap out-of-context Bible verses onto real problems. We will not offer quick fixes to entrenched challenges. Our world does not need another book promising simple solutions to complex problems.

We feature Jeremiah in this book, knowing literally nothing worked out as he hoped it would. Jeremiah and his contemporaries watched everything they cherished and hoped for crumble. Their leaders failed them. Their city walls no longer protected them. Their security, safety, and certainty evaporated. Their hope ran very thin. Many gave up on God. And no amount of positive thinking or inspirational Christian wall art promising a hope and a future would change their circumstances. Yet Jeremiah remained faithful and hopeful throughout his journey.

Whether you've been serving for years or are early on your journey, we pray the truth found in Scripture and the stories in these pages point you to the God of hope. To the God who sustained Jeremiah when the world imploded around him. To the God who guides and empowers the leaders you will meet in this book. And to the God who we believe is the only way to sustain your service, too.

We invite you to look away from the dire headlines and the discord on your newsfeed. To find respite and renewed strength as you journey with us in exploring stories of hope that will encourage you to get your hands a little dirtier, grow your faith a little deeper, and lift your gaze a little higher. To "hold tightly without wavering to the hope we affirm, for God can be trusted to keep his promise."[16]

Hope is not lost.

Application Questions

1. What experiences or stories have drained you of hope? What might this reveal about the source of your hope?
2. Which individuals or stories profiled in Scripture have enlivened your own hope?
3. On the journey from idealism to enduring hope, where do you currently find yourself?

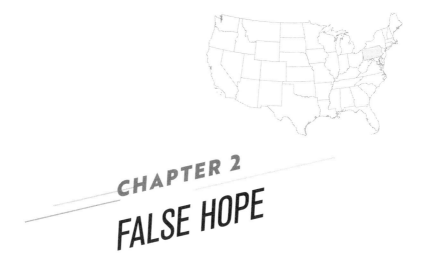

CHAPTER 2
FALSE HOPE

How wonderful it is that no one has to wait, but can start right now to gradually change the world! How wonderful it is that everyone, great and small, can immediately help bring about justice by giving of themselves!

—Anne Frank[1]

L et's do something."

My (Peter's) math was simple and my understanding of foster care naïve. In our region, 14,000 kids awaited a safe home and a loving family, and without too much difficulty our family could rearrange our home to make space for at least one more: 14,000 minus 1 seemed like a modest step in the right direction.

Our home had space. Our family had love. We could do this.

Confronted by the need—and unambiguous about God's heart for the orphan, the widow, or anyone in distress—we were ready to dive headfirst into the world of foster care.

While we didn't know all the details of how foster care worked, we knew this decision was right, good, and significant.

Several weeks later, we sat in a training session with other families beginning the journey of foster care or adoption. Most of the attendees found themselves in the same place as us: armed with the ardent conviction of our call to love and care for vulnerable children. Resolved to *do something*. Kids in crisis needed a safe space, and collectively we believed we could have a real impact. We shared a plate of graham crackers and a willingness to respond. Coffee filled our Styrofoam cups, and optimism brewed in our hearts.

As the training began, my eyes wandered to the photos around the room of sunsets, fields, barns, and beaches—each picture-perfect setting the backdrop for smiling families. We were on the cusp of *forever* changing the lives of vulnerable children in our community.

> **Idealism:** *our unrealistic and imaginative vision of the future; a false hope in guaranteed success.*

Idealism and a certain degree of naïveté have helped to change the world, for if we knew the full scope of challenges at the outset of any endeavor to love others, we might turn away, running fast and far. Idealism helps us to believe not only that challenges should be addressed but also that we should address them. It prompts us to take that first step. Idealism is full of promise and potential.

Anyone who has engaged in addressing the big challenges in our world has sipped from the optimist's half-full glass. We believe positive impact will result from the combination of the right inputs, creativity, and unconditional love.

We believe this change is not just *possible* but *probable*. With enough love, idealism assures us, every story has the potential of a happily-ever-after.

While often referred to as "youthful idealism," idealism is certainly not confined to the young. It shows up in the mid-career professional hoping to find a new, more rewarding career in the nonprofit sector. It buoys the professional who volunteers after work. It woos the family who signs up for foster care. It entices the international-trip participant eager to make a difference in the world. Idealism bolsters the board member willing to serve.

We desperately need people with such high hopes and ideals. We need people who see what God created this world to be and courageously respond, believing it's possible to make a positive impact. Nonprofit organizations, churches, and the service sector are disproportionately full of idealists.

Idealism sets lofty goals. Yet, left to its own devices, idealism presents a false hope. It makes promises that are impossible to keep.

All of us who engage in long-term service soon discover reality is in fact full of nuance, complications, and pain. For our family, it didn't take long to recognize the smiling snapshots of children and their families—beautifully photographed and framed for public display— did not tell the full story.

Over the next five years, twelve foster children lived in our home and made their way into our hearts. We experienced many beautiful moments, but this period also led to the single most painful season of our lives. We knew the saying that "hurt people hurt people," but we never anticipated the direct application of the words. Nothing has come close to the hurt, fear, and brokenness we felt. Rages that wouldn't stop. Emergency room visits. Feeling our family falling apart. Disturbing moments in police stations. Cameras installed in our home in an attempt to make us feel safe again. Baffling courtroom decisions. Organizations we trusted abandoning us when we needed them most. Wrenching goodbyes and the haunting feeling that we did not do enough.

We were not just hurt. We were wounded.

When we embarked on our foster-care journey, we understood that the stories of the children we would encounter often began with unspeakable pain. What we didn't anticipate was that sometimes our family's story with these precious children would also end with pain. Sometimes there would be no happily-ever-after to celebrate—no clear resolution, restoration, or healing. Sometimes we would love a child as deeply and fiercely as we could and still it would not be enough.

Most heartbreaking of all, I watched the people I loved the most become deeply wounded in the process. This was the end of our idealism.

Disillusionment: *a turning point when reality clashes with our expectations.*

In the midst of it all, we captured our own smiling photos of our temporarily enlarged family holding hands against beautiful backdrops. There were occasions when the system worked as it was designed to work, and families were reunited. We glimpsed restoration and joy and more beauty than words can articulate. Those redemptive moments were real, but so were the tangible, searing reminders of the depth of brokenness all around us. This journey was far more complex, demanding, and challenging than we could ever have anticipated.

After our most painful season when we felt hurt and betrayed, I hastily constructed walls around my heart.

I hated that so many of the precious kids in the foster-care system had already experienced more hurt, loss, and abandonment than most of us will ever be able to wrap our minds around.

I hated the maddening injustice of how some kids have been wounded by the very people who were supposed to love them best.

I hated the pain we experienced in opening our hearts and home. I hated even thinking that, as I knew our pain was just a fraction of what these children had endured.

I hated the mind-numbing complexity of navigating the difficult systems and cumbersome bureaucracies that seemed to fail vulnerable children.

I was disillusioned, as it felt impossible to really make an impact; the hurts were already too deep.

With the trauma-induced outbursts we couldn't seem to control, and the agency decisions we couldn't understand, was it worth it? At a particularly low point, I concluded, "We will never do this again." We were spent. We couldn't grit it out. It was simply too much. Too difficult. Too costly.

I wanted to walk—no, *run*—away. I wanted to lock the front door of our home and refuse to open it again. I wanted to insulate my family from the pain we experienced by finding "safer" and more sanitized ways of caring for our neighbors: loving them but from a more comfortable distance.

Cynicism started to invade the space once occupied by idealism.

Cynicism: *our disbelief that positive change is possible.*

I read books on grit and resilience, and they only intensified my feelings of inadequacy. Optimism was insufficient, and I couldn't keep trying harder or clinging tighter to a false hope that everything would eventually work out. The allure of cynicism as an "easy out" grew.

The system is too broken.
The kids are too hurt.
The process is beyond hope.
We are wasting our time.
This will never change.

During a difficult season, our family watched the remake of the 1977 Broadway musical *Annie*. Annie moves from a hard-knock life into a mansion, and everything is made right in the end. The soundtrack promises "the sun will come out tomorrow."² How simple—how empty—that promise seemed. What should we do when it's still raining? When the clouds shroud the sun day after day? When hope is elusive? When the happily-ever-after never arrives?

Cynicism offered a compelling alternative, inviting me to quit trying while also assuaging my guilt. It wasn't my lack of resolve or resilience that kept the sun from peeking through the clouds; it was the system . . . the families . . . the brokenness. My family and I could not make any difference at all in the lives of these families, so we might as well accept it and move on with our safety and sanity intact.

We've all heard that "failure is never final." But for many, it *is* final. Sometimes we find ourselves too bruised to get back up and keep fighting. Often at the pivot point of disillusionment, we question if it's time to give up.

Cynicism pulled at us strongly, and yet deep down we knew opting out was not the answer. Kids in need of a home didn't have the luxury of opting out; why should we?

How could we sustain service for the long term?

Enduring hope: *our complete trust and active expectation in God's redemptive work.*

With our most painful experiences still very raw, I met with Ann Saylor. We were involved with the same foster-care agency and connected at a church luncheon. I remember the applesauce and ham loaf served that day, perhaps because after two decades of living in Lancaster County, Pennsylvania, I still find ham loaf an oddity. But more memorable than the food was Ann's youthful demeanor and delight.

When I asked how many foster children she has welcomed into her home, she replied, "Somewhere around ninety." According to the agency, the actual number is 116.

"Ann, how do you keep going, especially when this journey of loving others really, really hurts?" I implored. That simple question allowed Ann to share her story and perspective on a path she has been walking for four decades.

Ann's demeanor seems incongruous with the reality of her story. It doesn't match the abuse she experienced as a child. It doesn't match the challenges she faced through a lifetime of loving kids in foster care. And it doesn't seem to match her age. At sixty-four, she is still opening her home with energy and enthusiasm.

As a child with eleven siblings, she defiantly told her mother that if they had one more sibling, she would run away from home. Ironic, since today she has welcomed ten times that number of children into her own home.

Ann shared that when she and her husband, Dennis, began as foster parents, they believed that love and nurturing a sense of belonging would heal all the hurts. They began as wide-eyed idealists.

"We were naïve," she laughs.

Over the course of a lifetime of service, Ann has been stretched beyond what she ever could have imagined.

There were more than a few moments in her foster-care journey when she considered giving up. She cared for kids who had experienced extreme trauma, including a twelve-year-old girl who would go into rages and turn her aggression toward Ann. She would pull Ann's hair mercilessly. When Ann called the agency for help, this girl bit her so hard that her arm turned black and blue from elbow to shoulder.

On multiple occasions, Ann hid the knives in the home and lived with the turmoil and unpredictability of physical harm. Ann and Dennis experienced the reality of trauma and the way it causes children to either fight, flee, or freeze. Through decades of caring for kids, she recalls vivid stories of children who responded in each of these ways.

Ann candidly shares about the seemingly impossible challenges they faced. "There were many times when I prayed, 'God, have you given me more than I can handle?'"

In reality, God had given her more than she could handle . . . on her own. There were times when it was all too much for her to carry. She reached the end of her abilities. But instead of turning inward, she turned upward. She looked to God as the One who fiercely loved these

"If we all gave up when it was hard, there would be no one left."

kids and empowered her to do the same. "If we all gave up when it was hard, there would be no one left," she summarizes.

So she kept on loving. She kept on opening her home. While there were seasons of respite, she reengaged. She remained hopeful, even when there were valid reasons to lose hope.

Instead of turning cynical, she turned upward to God and outward with compassion. Like many of the children who enter her home, Ann experienced abuse as a child. She believes that her horrific experiences cultivated her love and understanding of other children who have been hurt. She sees her own hurt and trauma as a bridge to connect more deeply to the children she chooses to love.

"I can't fully explain it," she shares, "but God always gave just enough love for the children placed in our home." Love flowed from Ann, and often it returned to her as well. During a difficult time in her life when Ann was diagnosed with breast cancer, the love of her foster children sustained her through the chemotherapy and recovery: "My kids were unquestionably part of my healing."

In talking to Ann, it's evident that her focus is not on herself. While she shares frankly about the pain and the many challenges, she speaks with God-given empathy and understanding for the children she serves. "If I were in their shoes, would I be able to pick up the pieces?" she asks.

Ann has been pushed to the limits but never turned to cynicism. She experienced disappointment and disillusionment but never turned inward. Somehow she weathered the storms with an informed hopefulness. A hopefulness that understands the hardships of the journey *and* likewise understands that God's grace is sufficient in our weakness.

While there are hurts, spending time with Ann means spending time hearing about the bonds and the breakthroughs. She shares about the opportunity to love and point people to God's grace. She shares the moment when one child was leaving her home and asked if he had to leave Jesus behind. Ann bent down and whispered, "You can take Jesus with you."

Friends have asked her, "How can you love someone else's child?" And her response is simple: "How can you not?"

Personally, and through the lives of these children, she has seen deep wounds but has remained hopeful that cycles can still be broken and hurts can be healed. Sometimes it comes at a cost, but Ann maintains hope in the power of Jesus to break through.

Pastor and theologian Timothy Keller describes biblical hope as "being certain about the future in a way that affects how you live now."[3] This life-altering hope sustains Ann's service. "I am not going to let challenges destroy or define me," she states, resolute in hope rooted in God's grace. Asked why she has given her life to this, Ann summarizes, "This is what Christ calls us to. And love comes with it."

There is duty. There is love. There is a steadfast commitment to caring for kids. And there is a confident and grounded hope in Christ.

Preparing for the Journey

This journey from idealism to disillusionment to enduring hope certainly isn't confined to foster care. It's an inevitable journey for all who serve.

It's a journey that leads people like Ann through disappointments, setbacks, and hurts. Even when there seem to be overwhelming reasons to give up, enduring hope sustains a lifetime of faithful service. So, let's prepare for a journey that will be far more difficult, and possibly far more beautiful, than we could dare to imagine.

For anyone eager to serve, lead, and make an impact in our world, seasons of discouragement are inevitable. There will be moments when we question our calling and consider giving up. Bill Massaquoi, founder of Rebuild Africa, attests: "What I discovered is that idealism can come to an end."

Theologian Eugene Peterson agrees. "Some people as they grow up become less. As children they have glorious ideas of who they are and of what life has for them. Thirty years later we find that they have settled for something grubby and inane. What accounts for the exchange of childhood aspiration to the adult anemia?"[4]

Without the sustaining force of idealism, some people shrink and become less: smaller dreams, smaller hopes, smaller goals. Their love, passion, and dreams grow cold. We don't want that to be our story. We want to retain the very best of youthful ideals while shedding the false promise of idealism. We want to passionately pursue goals that exceed our personal capacity—and never settle for the inane. To not drift to lukewarmness or apathy, but to find ways of living with enduring hope and expectation.

When we reach the end of idealism, where do we turn to restore our hope?

Application Questions

1. Why does it seem that nonprofit organizations, churches, and the service sector are disproportionately full of idealists?

2. What has been the role of idealism in your own life? When has it proved insufficient?
3. How does God use our seasons of idealism?
4. What are the dangers of idealism?
5. How does idealism differ from enduring hope?

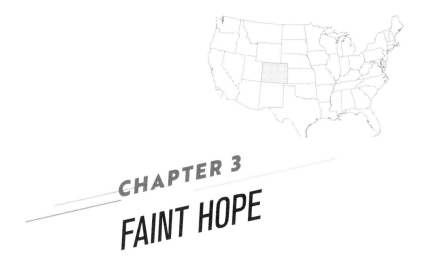

CHAPTER 3
FAINT HOPE

> Disillusionment is a gift, because it is a sign we were living in illusionment.
>
> —John Mark Comer[1]

(Chris) woke up early after a fitful night. I did not want to be awake so early, but sleep eluded me.

In an act of resignation, I brewed the first of the day's several pots of coffee. I opened my phone and began to pore over apocalyptic headlines. It was March 16, 2020, and the prevailing opinion was clear: COVID-19 *was upending everything. Hospitals would be overrun. Millions would die. Economies would crumble. Normalcy had evaporated.* I am a mostly unflinching optimist. But that morning, a heavy reality came crashing down upon me. *This is going to be the worst thing I've ever experienced.*

Disillusionment: *a turning point when reality clashes with our expectations.*

That morning marked the beginning of a five-month valley: easily the worst season of my career. At HOPE International, I lead an incredible team of people advancing our mission to invest in the dreams of families in the world's underserved communities as we proclaim and live the gospel. We share the hope of Christ as we provide biblically based training, savings services, and loans that restore dignity and break the cycle of poverty. I love what I do. Ordinarily. But not from March through August 2020. For that season, my work was laborious—even on the best days.

Everyone had an opinion about how bad the pandemic would be. Donors, board members, coworkers, and friends passed along their blueprints for survival. Each journal article and essay featured its own flavor of awful. Nearly everyone recommended we cancel everything, cut back budgets to the bone, begin layoffs, and prepare to hunker down for years.

Prior to 2020, none of us had lived through a public health emergency of this sort. We saw no option but to prepare for bad, worse, and cataclysmic potential futures. We fumbled blindly along, attempting to lead wisely amid what felt like a dense fog.

Pandemic fatigue hit our leaders and departments in waves, often taking us sideways. It surprised me when I found myself growing frustrated even with my boss (yes, the same boss who is coauthoring this book!), a very rare occurrence in our tenure working together. Stress bubbled up everywhere.

At home, things weren't much better. With four children under the age of ten, my wife and I saw *a lot* of them during the extended lockdown. For the first time in my adult life, I had *too much* family togetherness. Without school, church, sports, and just about everything else, we fought to hold on to our sanity. We love our children immensely. But parenting a brood of small kids during a pandemic is not something I would wish upon anyone.

Eventually I ran out of optimism. My hope grew faint. And at that inflection point, I grew weary and increasingly disillusioned.

Doomscrolling

A few months into the pandemic, my wife, Alli, and I put our kids to bed and then sat together on our front porch. I shared something aloud that I had been feeling privately for a while.

"I think I might be depressed."

This revelation did not surprise her. Over the course of the previous months, I had been distant, withdrawn, and emotionally flat. I was often lost in my own thoughts, my mind turning over the latest research or lockdown stories I had just read. I devoured the news, often spending hours each day reading and assessing the latest outlook.

I knew it wasn't helping, but I couldn't stop doomscrolling. I woke up in the middle of many nights feeling panicked and agitated about the state of the world.

The steady, everyday stress began to eat away at my hope. The what-ifs consumed my thoughts. I was demoralized and discouraged much of the time, even if I attempted to assure myself that God had everything under control. Yet I lost all appetite for prayer, and the Bible seemed distant and cold.

The leadership journey can be deeply isolating. For the first time in my career, I really felt this. I wanted to inspire hope in my team. I wanted to cast a compelling vision for our donors. But I struggled to believe the very things I said to them. My self-diagnosis was not clinical, but from what I knew of depression, this was the closest I'd ever come to it.

As the months wore on, the grind and low-grade anxiety from pressures both big and small began to steal my hope. With each passing week, I found myself increasingly dreaming about quitting my job and moving to a cabin somewhere deep in the mountains west of our home in Denver, Colorado. The challenges surrounding my family and my work felt insurmountable. I wanted to pull the plug and homestead somewhere off the grid.

Grapeless Vines

My 2020 trajectory—like many others', I'm told—was not good. I reached a point midsummer when I realized I needed to take an honest assessment of where I found myself. Whenever we reach the place where our hope grows faint, we face the choice of turning inward and attempting to white-knuckle our way through our pain. The pain in our lives can push us toward cynicism.

Or we can follow the path of Habakkuk, a contemporary of Jeremiah.

Habakkuk wrote in lament of how God's people abandoned their first love. He saw his country held captive while Babylon destroyed the nation. He wrote when everything was falling apart. When nothing made sense. When God seemed silent and distant. When his confidence in God wavered.

Habakkuk stated it this way:

> Even though the fig trees have no blossoms,
>   and there are no grapes on the vines;
> even though the olive crop fails,
>   and the fields lie empty and barren;
> even though the flocks die in the fields,
>   and the cattle barns are empty . . .

Habakkuk didn't understand. There were no grapes or olives. The fields were empty. I love the honest prayers of the Old Testament prophets. Habakkuk and Jeremiah do not trivialize their desperation by bookending their laments, saying "everything happens for a reason." Their anguish is palpable. Often overlooked in American Christianity, lament gives us space to grieve the brokenness around us, to cry out to God when things are not as they should be.[2] Author Soong-Chan Rah writes in his book *Prophetic Lament*, "Lament challenges the church to acknowledge real suffering and plead with God for his intervention."[3]

Jeremiah authored an *entire book of the Bible* with his laments. There is nothing glib about his prayers or the prayers of his contemporary, Habakkuk. But neither do they remain in their misery. Even as they waver in their confidence in God's goodness, they remind themselves of what is true. Habakkuk continues,

> . . . yet I will rejoice in the LORD!
>   I will be joyful in the God of my salvation!
> The Sovereign LORD is my strength!
>   He makes me as surefooted as a deer,
>   able to tread upon the heights.[4]

He does not define his fulfillment by his circumstances.

Is it possible to turn upward to God even when we don't want to? When we're frustrated and depressed? Habakkuk seemed to think so. And the resulting surefootedness is something I longed for in my own life.

Mountain biking is my favorite of Colorado's many outdoor sports. But if there's one thing I've learned from crashing while traversing singletrack trails across the state (more times than I care to admit!), it's this: The very worst thing you can do while navigating rocks, roots, and puddles is look down.

To conquer dicey trails, I need to fight the urge to look down and instead look out. The key to a great ride is to fix my vision farther down the trail, not down at my tires. Likewise, fixing our vision on God—especially during hard times and in the moments we feel little desire to do so—allows us to journey, as Habakkuk writes, "as sure-footed as a deer."[5]

In this season of disillusionment, I longed for enduring hope. But I looked for it in the wrong places.

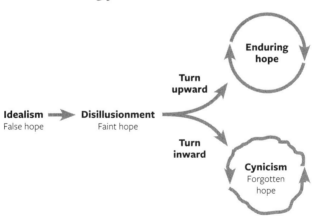

Inward or Upward?

In a pandemic or any other crisis, there is a noticeable difference between those who turn inward and those who turn upward and outward. Those who are preoccupied by fear and loss versus those who are actively and intentionally looking beyond themselves—upward to God and outward to their neighbors. Those who hoard supplies and those who show up to share what they have. Those who lock their doors and close the blinds and those who open their arms and hearts to others in more challenging circumstances.

Psychologist Daniel Goleman writes, "Self-absorption in all its forms kills empathy, let alone compassion. When we focus on ourselves, our world contracts as our problems and preoccupations loom large. But when we focus on others, our world expands. Our own problems drift to the periphery of the mind and so seem smaller, and we increase our capacity for connection—or compassionate action."[6]

Like Habakkuk, I saw problems all around me. But unlike him, I found myself completely absorbed by all that was going wrong. With the world on lockdown, I gave myself permission to opt out of the things that mattered most. I withdrew from friends who knew me well. I complained more and prayed less.

That all began to change on a Friday night that August.

Right before dinnertime, our school district notified us they would be indefinitely postponing the resumption of in-person education. For us, the return of school was our pandemic finish line. We *needed* our kids to get into classrooms with their teachers and fellow students. This news sucked away our remaining vestiges of hope.

Alli and I began to process aloud what this would mean for our jobs, our schedules, and our sanity. We hated that our children would miss months more of school. We hated that this miserable season was not coming to the conclusion we imagined.

But at some point in the evening, our perspective began to shift. We knew we needed to make a big change.

By the end of the night, we had made our decision: We would launch a quasi-school—Wildside Academy—in our backyard for our kids and eight kids from our neighborhood. To be honest, we did not have overtly spiritual intentions with this decision. We did not hear God's voice audibly tell us to launch a school. We were simply fed up with being fed up.

As we reflect on the decision, we know God called us to take this step. In retrospect we can see how desperately we needed to get beyond ourselves. But in the moment, all we knew was that our habitual sulking wasn't working. And no amount of positive thinking, yoga, or clean eating was going to fix anything either.

Yes, we had lots of justifiable things to complain about, but we also had all sorts of opportunities, that is, if we were willing to shift our gaze beyond ourselves.

Though the postponement of in-person school was inconvenient for us, we began to consider how damaging it would be for families who lacked our levels of wealth, privilege, and work flexibility. The evidence of this was indisputable: Based on surveys from Los Angeles, Boston, and even South Dakota, we learned that more than 20% of public-school students were not even signing on to their virtual school platforms.[7] This 20% dropout rate has had a devastating impact on the children and families least able to bounce back. After making the decision to launch a backyard school, we asked our school administrators which families were experiencing the most pain from the closure of our public school. They referred several families to us. One family were refugees, and the parents struggled to navigate the online portals because they did not speak English as a first language.

One mom we called to invite to join Wildside Academy works nights and had a hard time getting her daughter engaged in virtual school. She bluntly summarized her experience with virtual school by saying, "It's been hell for us."

A few weeks later, we welcomed her daughter, seven other children, and our two oldest kids to Wildside Academy, a backyard "microschool" for our neighborhood. Over the next few months these ten students gathered three days a week in our yard to learn, play, and adventure together. We did not charge tuition and had no idea if our experiment would work. In the least important ways, it was challenging. Managing ten children's Wi-Fi connections, usernames and passwords, and laptop-charging issues is nothing short of a hot mess. But in the most important ways, it was one of the best things we'd ever done. We would do it all over again.

These students loved coming to Wildside. We loved the students and loved being *in it* with their families. We grew in our empathy for our school's teachers and administrators. Our friends and families joined us by donating supplies and snacks to Wildside. And for me personally, it replaced my discouraged self-pity with God-given mission, purpose, and meaning. The gift of disillusionment was that it shifted my vision from myself to how God wanted to move in this challenging situation.

Beyond Ourselves

"Our disillusionment is not a bad thing," writes theologian Barbara Brown Taylor. "Take the word apart and you can begin to hear what it really means. Dis-illusion-ment. The loss of illusion. The end of make-believe. Is that a bad thing? Or a good thing? To learn that God's presence is not something we can demand, that God's job is not to reward our devotion, that God's agenda may in fact be quite different from our own. Is that a bad thing or a good thing to know?"[8]

Amid the pandemic, my idealism failed me. My hope grew faint. I could not fight my way out of the pandemic. I could not try harder or employ the latest leadership tactic to fix things. Aimless, self-absorbed,

> God invited me to let go of this illusion: that peace in my circumstances and the environment would lead to peace in my heart.

and preoccupied, I careened toward cynicism. But it was in this disillusionment that God intervened. God invited me to let go of this illusion: that peace in my circumstances and the environment would lead to peace in my heart.

It had become my pattern during those valley months to obsess about all that was wrong with the world, all that was wrong with our politics, all that was wrong at work and at home. But as I dwelled on all these massive problems I couldn't wish or work my way out of, ironically my world became smaller and smaller. My biggest problem was self-preoccupation. Wildside Academy became an on-ramp to remembering God's faithfulness and an off-ramp to my burgeoning cynicism.

Each afternoon at Wildside Academy, we'd find a shady spot in which to stretch out and relax after a day of schoolwork for "book club," and I would read *The Giver* aloud to a group of our oldest students. In the middle of book club one day, Daniel interrupted me to share some of his story.[9] Daniel shared with me and his classmates that he had escaped the Republic of Congo as a refugee and lived in Malawi for a few years prior to moving to Colorado.

He shared about how he still struggled with pronouncing some words in English. He talked about how grateful he was for his family and the challenges they had overcome together. I sat and listened, engrossed in Daniel's story. This was one remarkable kid. I was so grateful we had the privilege of knowing him, of welcoming him into our backyard each day. Over the two months we hosted Wildside Academy, the more time I spent with Daniel, the less time I spent disillusioned. Following God's invitation to look to Him allowed me to love neighbors like Daniel. And slowly, this step of looking upward to God led me to look outward to my neighbors, and this journey began to renew my hope.

Wildside Academy was a very small step toward following Habak-kuk's lead and turning upward to God with our honest frustration. It was a first step in turning away from ourselves. It was not a cure-all. It did not vanquish my disillusionment overnight. It did not right the personal and systemic challenges facing our family, our community, and the world. We were still tired all the time. The pandemic raged on.

But it subtly yet substantially shifted our hearts and imaginations. And this shift, multiplied over several months, helped to reorient our preoccupations. With each day that passed, we became a bit less ab-sorbed in our own lives and more caught up in the beauty of what God was doing around us.

The journey to cynicism accelerates when we grow preoccupied with the wrong things. A crisis tempts us to turn inward, but it also invites us to expand our worlds, to share our unfiltered complaints with God, to grow our compassion, and, in the process, to turn upward and notice how our problems and preoccupations become smaller as we do. If we're open to it, we can be reminded of God's provision—even in a crisis—and, from that place of confidence in God's provision, extend that provision to those around us.

What if we all think about ourselves a little less? What if we give ourselves the gift of getting over ourselves? Habakkuk looked beyond his circumstances and reminded himself that God never fails. That God can renew our hope.

Though disillusionment may be the inevitable outcome of our expectations and experiences colliding, what follows hinges on our decision to turn inward or upward.

Application Questions

1. When have you experienced disillusionment? How did you feel?
2. How can something as painful as disillusionment be a gift?
3. In trying situations, is your natural inclination to turn inward or upward?
4. What illusions have you already lost? What illusions is God calling you to let go of?

CHAPTER 4
FORGOTTEN HOPE

Our task, as image-bearing, God-loving, Christ-shaped, Spirit-filled Christians, following Christ and shaping our world, is to announce redemption to the world that has discovered its fallenness . . . to announce healing to a world that has discovered its brokenness, to proclaim love and trust to the world that knows only exploitation, fear, and suspicion.

—N. T. Wright[1]

Accepting the role of General Superintendent Emerita of the Wesleyan Church to the cheers and applause of her peers, Dr. Jo Anne Lyon bowed her head humbly, tears filling her eyes. After serving as the general superintendent for eight years, she admitted, "This is a title I never in my wildest dreams thought I would have." Her voice quavering with emotion, Jo Anne went on to share a summary of her own faith journey and her sometimes tumultuous relationship with the Church.[2]

The daughter of pastors and evangelists who planted over a dozen churches, Jo Anne narrowly avoided being born at a tent revival meeting. It would have been a start befitting a young girl who would spend so much of her time in church and ministry. "I grew up with a great love for the Church," she recalls.[3]

She was raised in a small, segregated town in Oklahoma in the 1940s, and Jo Anne's awareness of injustice and inequality began to take shape early. When she was just five years old, she saw a woman picking up trash in her neighborhood. Jo Anne was intrigued—this was the first black woman she had ever seen. The woman returned every Wednesday morning, collecting trash and singing as she worked.

"Where does that woman live?" Jo Anne asked her father. "And why doesn't she come to our church?" To answer her questions, her father agreed to take her for a drive to the woman's neighborhood.

"I'll never forget that day," Jo Anne remarks. She and her father drove to a place Jo Anne hadn't even known existed. At the border separating the white community from the black, the pavement ended and a dirt road began. It wasn't just the road; this place was geographically close but far removed from her own neighborhood in almost every way. In fact, some "houses" were just tar-paper shanties.

Confused, Jo Anne again asked her father why these people didn't come to their church or their school. Her father responded simply, "They have their own church and their own school."

"But those answers never satisfied me," Jo Anne shares.

Holy, Not Just

Two decades later, at the height of the Civil Rights movement in the 1960s, Jo Anne and her husband, Wayne, moved to Missouri, where Wayne attended seminary and Jo Anne completed a graduate degree in counseling. Together they planted a Wesleyan church in Kansas City in 1968.

A few weeks later, in their very own city, riots erupted, spurred by the assassination of Dr. Martin Luther King Jr. and frustration over the agonizingly slow pace of progress. Stirred by the call for justice, Jo Anne and Wayne joined the protesters. Surely the Church she had loved all her life could speak into this crisis with wisdom and authority.

Yet the Church remained silent, and their congregation wanted no role in the protests—even if they were peaceful and just.

Historically, the Wesleyan Church had been known for its influential role in the abolitionist movement, but in recent years church leaders had disconnected faith from social action. "We became isolated and inward, just trying to be holy, not realizing that a life of holiness embraces issues of justice," Jo Anne says.

Jo Anne recognized that fear was causing the Church's world to grow smaller, as their focus on self-preservation loomed larger. Discontent, she continued to call the Church to outward-focused action, but her pleas fell upon deaf ears.

Cynicism: *our disbelief that positive change is possible.*

The hypocrisy of an apathetic Church proclaiming love of God and neighbors became overwhelming to Jo Anne. It grated on her. In the Church's silence and inaction in the face of injustice, Jo Anne perceived complicity. The Church refused to act on matters that so clearly mattered to God. If this was the body of Christ, it had become paralyzed.

Her disappointment in the Wesleyan Church—an institution she loved—morphed into disdain. "I didn't like to go to church, frankly, and I didn't like the people." Over dinner one night, she pleaded with Wayne to leave pastoral ministry and the church. She remembers suggesting he instead employ his winsome personality to sell insurance and use the profits to serve God. Clear in his calling, Wayne responded, "I don't know what you're going to do, Jo Anne, but God's called me to preach, and that's what I have to do."[4]

Their relationship became strained as Jo Anne made no secret of her disapproval of this calling.

She vividly recalls returning home one evening after a day of work as a teacher and hearing God prompt her to get her spiritual life in order. "Well, it will have to be in February because I have to get [the church's] Christmas program together right now," she snapped back.[5]

As she spoke into the Church's hypocrisy from the firm ground of moral certitude, pride blinded Jo Anne to the dangerous trajectory her own heart was taking. She had grown cynical toward the Church she once loved.

Surgical Intervention

At one point, Jo Anne fell ill. It wasn't the type of "illness" that had recently plagued her only on Sunday mornings, just long enough to avoid church services. On this particular morning, her stomach ached so severely she couldn't get off the floor. Wayne drove her to the hospital. "As I was being rolled into that hospital, I thought, 'Well, I guess I'm in here to witness to someone.' You know how you can just be such a professional Christian?" she says, her voice thick with irony. God *was* prompting, but not in the way she expected. "The words of that old hymn came back. 'It's not your brother or your sister, but it's *you* standing in the need of prayer.'"[6]

As Jo Anne anticipated surgery and an extended hospital stay, Wayne urged her to read a book he had often suggested: Catherine Marshall's *Beyond Ourselves*. "But I was just so convinced that I didn't need to read it," she says. "My pride prevented me from seeing that [Marshall] had anything to teach me."

Nevertheless, out of boredom and perhaps desperation, Jo Anne finally picked up the book and began to read. When she came to a chapter on ego, the Holy Spirit convicted her. She repented of her arrogance, pride, unforgiveness, and anger. And suddenly, for the first time in her life, she became hungry for God. "I wanted God more than anything else in this world," she recalls.

Soon after, doctors concluded there was nothing wrong with Jo Anne's stomach. She wouldn't need the surgery doctors had predicted after all, and she was free to go home. "I realized that God had done surgery on my heart, and we didn't need to do surgery on my stomach."[7]

Later that week, Wayne was traveling, so he asked Jo Anne to lead a prayer meeting at the church. She hungered for God, but she was still frustrated with the Church and made it clear to both Wayne and God that she didn't want to go.

When no one else volunteered, she grudgingly agreed to lead. During the prayer meeting, the congregants started singing the lyrics of an old hymn: "Hallelujah, I have found Him, the One Whom my soul has craved." And that night, the Holy Spirit came over Jo Anne in ways she can't describe. She began confessing to the people in the prayer meeting her reactions toward the Church, toward *them*. "As I confessed, suddenly, I was so filled with love for people that night that I could not contain myself. . . . I had love for those people I could not will myself to love—and that changed the course of my life entirely."

Jo Anne felt God's love uprooting cynicism in her own life. She felt an all-new source of hope. Jo Anne had been looking for hope in the Church rather than in God.

Her misplaced hope resonates. When we encounter church leaders obsessed with political ideologies or abusing their power or practicing all flavors of hypocrisy, we're ready to join Jo Anne in writing off the

> In a paradoxical way, cynicism appears to be the plague of what others are or are not doing. But at its core, cynicism is a byproduct of pride.

Church. When the next scandal makes headlines, we feel our hope eroding. We feel a sense of personal superiority bubbling up within us, our anger at the new injustice seeding our growing cynicism. In a paradoxical way, cynicism appears to be the plague of what *others* are or are not doing. But at its core, cynicism is a byproduct of pride. It is a disbelief that positive change is possible based on our assessment of our own strength to enact that positive change. Yet in the operating room of Jo Anne's heart, God revealed He was the only reliable source of enduring hope.

Holy and Just

After a move to Grand Rapids, Michigan, Jo Anne discovered a community of friends who shared her passion to see the Church engage in gospel-centered social justice. Alongside an ecumenical group, Jo Anne began researching how the Church might combat the problem of global hunger. An ABC News team recognized her efforts and invited her to travel to Ethiopia to help film a documentary on a famine ravaging the country.

On the ground in Ethiopia, Jo Anne met individuals from Japan, Holland, and countless other countries. The world seemed to be showing up to respond to the crisis—but the Church was conspicuously absent.

Returning home, Jo Anne confronted Wesleyan leaders. "We need to do something!"

They dismissed her entreaties: "We are just about evangelism and church planting."

"But people are dying," she said.

"They'll go to heaven," came the callous reply.

Once again cynicism beckoned. How could followers of Christ be so hardhearted toward those in need? She was asking the modern-day equivalent of a question first asked by the apostle John two thousand years ago, "If someone has enough money to live well and sees a brother or sister in need but shows no compassion—how can God's love be in that person?"[8]

Though the Church is called to be the body of Christ, Jo Anne began to recognize that it is not immune from the brokenness of our world. It can be a place where sinners find grace and peace, but it can also be a place where followers become wounded and disillusioned, and faith falters. Many see the shortcomings of the Church and give up not only on church but on faith altogether. Many conflate God and the institution.

Yet God grieves when the Church is complacent, when politics matter more than people, when the priorities of the Church blatantly disregard the priorities of the One they seek to represent. The Church's failures and shortcomings undoubtedly breed cynicism, yet the Church was never intended to be the ultimate source of our hope. Like the prophet Jeremiah, Jo Anne refused to succumb to cynicism and instead said, "We set our hope on you."[9] Those who hope in the Church will grow disillusioned and eventually cynical, but "those who hope in the LORD will renew their strength."[10]

Jo Anne channeled her disillusionment differently this time. She turned upward to God: the God who cared for the hungry and hurting even more than she did. She did not conflate the actions of apathetic people in the Church with the One who paid the price for all the apathetic and inward-focused. Initially, she heard a simple invitation to explore what she *could* do. She focused less on her disappointment with others and more on actions she could take.

"[Leaders] have seen, and borne, the worst that institutions can do—and yet they have somehow escaped the abyss of cynicism," writes Andy Crouch in his book *Playing God*. "Instead they enter into the life of their institutions, embodying a better way, bearing the institution's pain and offering hope."[11]

Instead of critiquing the Church for inaction, Jo Anne took action by teaching about the importance of pairing holiness and justice. She emphasized Amos 5:24 (ESV): "But let justice roll down like waters, and righteousness like an ever-flowing stream." With zeal, she shared that holiness and justice fit together; they could not be separated. She reminded congregations that in addressing issues of social justice, they weren't tossing out evangelism and church planting; rather, they would be coming alongside people in need, empowering them to do their own evangelism and church planting in their own countries.

She prayed, she worked, she waited, and all the while God sustained a vision in her heart for the Church to bring the Great Commission and the greatest commandments together.

Jo Anne discovered the beauty of the "fullness of time." In hindsight, she sees that, like cultivating before a harvest, God needed to prepare her for the work He intended for her to do. With young children at home, Jo Anne preferred not to travel extensively. She also had much to learn about development work and the nonprofit sector, as well as the internal work of shoring up her own theological base and learning to handle conflict and criticism.

In 1993, when a new leader—with a similar vision to Jo Anne's—joined the missions team at the Wesleyan Church, he and Jo Anne started to discuss what it could look like to engage the church in holiness and justice. The result was World Hope International, which Jo Anne founded in the back bedroom of a parsonage in January 1996.

Launching World Hope International

Though the Wesleyan Church was supportive of the new ministry—a welcome change from their response a decade earlier—they didn't have any capital to offer.

Neither was Jo Anne's family in a position to financially support the burgeoning organization. At the time, two of her four children were in college. Wayne was still pastoring, and Jo Anne was working as the clinical director for the county's mental health system. She felt discouraged and constrained by the lack of financial resources.

That December, as she read the Christmas story, she asked God for fresh insight. As she read the familiar words of the angel Gabriel, they jumped off the page afresh: "For nothing will be impossible with God."[12]

Mary's response was just as powerful: "I am the Lord's servant. . . . May your word to me be fulfilled."[13]

"That's it," Jo Anne decided. "I am the Lord's servant. Let's go."

In an enormous leap of faith, she resigned from her clinical director role. When she did, her supervisor, thinking she was crazy, told her that they'd keep her job vacant for at least a month, so she would have something to fall back on.

"Well," Jo Anne quips with a smile, "it's been twenty-five years now."

A few weeks after Jo Anne handed in her resignation, her husband called her from the church office. "I'm working on the finances," he said. "And I know God's going to do something, but when will you get your last paycheck?"

Her final paycheck arrived on January 20. Shortly thereafter, Jo Anne met with a business leader. When she shared World Hope's first-year operations budget, the man looked it over and, as if the Spirit of God came over him, replied in tears, "Our family will pick up the whole thing."

Over the next few months, God continued to confirm the establishment of World Hope. Friends and strangers alike donated funds to get the organization off the ground. With an emphasis on relief and development work, Jo Anne and her team set foot in war-torn regions, abandoned communities, and red-light districts to equip individuals with opportunity and the hope of Christ.

There were many times that Jo Anne didn't think they'd be able to meet their budget. One night, unsure of how they were going to provide promised funds for individuals in the middle of the Liberian Civil War, she raised her hands to heaven and declared, "Lord, You care about the situation and people in Liberia more than we do. We need Your help. We cannot do it anymore. Yet *nothing is impossible with You*." And the very next morning, she received a phone call from a stranger who wanted to help.

"God is in the redemption business, and He's called us to partner with Him in bringing redemption and seeing nations changed," Jo Anne shares. "This has nothing to do with our power and everything to do with the power of God."

Beyond the financial challenges, there were some who resisted the fact that a woman was leading the organization. After Jo Anne preached and shared about World Hope in one church, the pastor brashly told her, "I just need you to know that I don't believe in women in leadership."

Instead of becoming defensive, she invited the pastor to read a book with her on the topic of women in ministry. She did not shut the door to the relationship but engaged in additional conversations. A decade later, this same pastor is one of Jo Anne's most ardent supporters. "Relationship is stronger than argument most of the time," Jo Anne says.

For the last twenty-five years, World Hope has provided "opportunity, dignity, and hope" for hundreds of thousands of families in need in over thirty countries, "so they can possess the tools for change in themselves, their families, and their community."[14] The organization focuses on a variety of different fronts, including clean water and energy, global health care, human rights services, and social ventures. Just as important, it is an example of how gospel proclamation and demonstration fit together. "A cup of cold water poured in the name of Jesus is a different kind of cup of water," Jo Anne shares.

Avoiding Cynicism

Jo Anne had every reason to grow—and stay—cynical with the Church. She witnessed racial injustice, experienced gender discrimination, and saw the Church turn a blind eye to suffering. She saw apathy and inaction in the face of massive global needs.

Yet in spending time with Jo Anne at Houghton College for a commencement weekend in 2019, I (Peter) saw no hint of cynicism. Instead, there was true joy, hope, and delight as she engaged with college students and called them to a life of active service. Instead of bitterness or resentment, she exuded enduring hope and deep love for everyone she met.

The last few years have felt like an echo of the turbulence Jo Anne and the Church experienced in the '60s. Churches rip apart from their own dysfunction. Some pastors ignore the Scriptures that challenge their politics. Others abandon the Scriptures altogether. Some ministry leaders wield their power to victimize those they should be serving. Other ministry leaders remain silent when they see it happening. Our

> **Our moment is not the first or the last turbulent season confronting the Church, but this moment is one where we find ourselves putting our hope in the wrong places.**

moment is not the first or the last turbulent season confronting the Church, but this moment is one where we find ourselves putting our hope in the wrong places.

But what I saw in Jo Anne was a leader who winsomely focused on activating the next generation of servant leaders, placing her hope in Christ alone. She implored them to not give up or give in to cynicism when they encounter disillusionment but rather to choose lives of faith and service.

"At a grassroots level, we need to figure out, as the people of God, how to lead in these crucial social issues of our day," Jo Anne remarks.

Through her life and her words, Jo Anne is working to ensure that the Church never again separates gospel witness and social action. She's committed to seeing the Church become a faithful presence and witness in our world.

Instead of just tolerating the Church with all its flaws, Jo Anne found a way to love the Church even while calling out its flaws. She did not stay silent when power was used for personal benefit. When people were hurt and the Church was silently complicit in the injustice. When the Church became stagnant, inward-focused, or apathetic to the needs of the world.

"A church that sits idly on the sideline when there is a fire is not a church that I want to be a part of," Jo Anne reflects. "It's misaligned with the greatest commandments to love God and to love our neighbors. It erodes our credibility to a watching world, causing people to question the God we purport to serve."

She moved forward in reform, empowered by God's Spirit, and guided by love—for those within the Church as well as for those outside it. "If your heart isn't broken for people, it doesn't matter what you do. We can't conjure love; deep love only comes from God."

Jo Anne is convinced that none of her work would have been possible without the indwelling of the Holy Spirit: "We can't live a holy life without the power of the Holy Spirit in us—to cleanse us, to fill us, to empower us."

Jo Anne models extraordinary commitment, hopefulness, and resilience. She overcame cynicism when she turned upward, gaining the courage to move forward in a broken world and the perspective to see God making things new.[15]

Today, in her eighties, Jo Anne still engages the Church with a contagious hopefulness on issues of racism and global poverty. She believes that just as the turbulence in the 1960s eventually gave way to the Jesus Movement in the 1970s, there is a movement in store for the Church today as hearts turn to Christ and to the mission Christ gave us.

Although many view this as a dark and difficult season, Jo Anne believes it is a moment not for cynicism but for hope. A moment to recapture a faith that is inextricably linked to action. A moment not to pull back or to give up but to look upward to the One who sustains our service.

Application Questions

1. Why might cynicism be a contagion?
2. What have you observed of cynical leaders?
3. When has pain, apathy, or hypocrisy pushed you toward cynicism?
4. How does our pride contribute to cynicism?

CHAPTER 5
UPWARD

We prefer our own wisdom to God's wisdom, our own desires to God's will, and our own reputation to God's honor. . . . The human heart is indeed a factory that mass-produces idols.

—Timothy Keller[1]

Throughout the Bible we read of the shocking prevalence of idolatry. Despite God's desire for proximity and relationship, time and again Israel traded the real thing for a counterfeit, turning away from the Living God toward golden cows, poles, or wooden carvings. It's tempting to scoff at their worship of inanimate objects. Jeremiah scornfully derided these men and women as "stupid and foolish."[2] Yet today our hearts remain equally capable of idol worship, and we suspect Jeremiah's blunt descriptors apply just as well to modern idolatry. Though we aren't bowing to statues or poles, we'd argue from personal experience that the temptation to idolize our own abilities lures many leaders. We put our faith in the gift of our abilities or intelligence rather than the Giver as we attempt to take on the intractable issues of our day in our own strength. Jeremiah's ancient words to the people of Judah resonate with contemporary truth as he calls out their idols—and ours—and offers an alternative.

Tumbleweeds and Fruit-Bearing Trees

In Jeremiah 17:5–6, God leads us into the dirt, providing, through Jeremiah, an agricultural object lesson.

This is what the Lord says:

> "Cursed are those who put their trust in mere humans,
>   who rely on human strength
>   and turn their hearts away from the LORD.
> They are like stunted shrubs in the desert,
>   with no hope for the future.
> They will live in the barren wilderness,
>   in an uninhabited salty land."

Cursed. Stunted. Barren. The image is bleak. God gives us a picture of unfulfilled promise: a living thing created to flourish but rooted in its own deficiency. Eugene Peterson's *The Message* says, "Cursed is the strong one . . . who thinks he can make it on muscle alone and sets GOD aside as dead weight. He's like a tumbleweed on the prairie, out of touch with the good earth. He lives rootless and aimless in a land where nothing grows."[3]

Tumbleweeds dot the landscape of the American West, showing up in film and folklore as a foreboding sign of isolation. When winter arrives, the brittle plants die, detach from their roots, and aimlessly blow wherever the wind carries them. Jeremiah observed God's people growing out of touch, picking the wrong soil, putting down roots not in God but in idols and illusions that couldn't sustain them. Jeremiah relates this image of the stunted shrub or the aimless tumbleweed to those who choose to sink their hopes in anything but God.

Most temptingly today, we place our confidence in the soil of self-reliance. With clenched teeth and gritty resolve, we say, *I've got this*. We believe ourselves qualified and capable, turning inward toward whatever resolve and resilience we can muster. It's pride and, Jeremiah would suggest, idolatry. We bow to the idol of our own abilities. But this type of humanism falters when the winds of pain and disappointment blow. Our good intentions can never be good enough to sustain us for the long term. Through the prophet Jeremiah, God invites us to pursue the alternative of "in my own strength" humanism: hopefulness, rooted in trust and active expectation in God's strength and faithfulness. He invites us to sustain hope amid the drought because He is the One who sustains. He invites us to cultivate deep roots that reach the ever-flowing Source of living water.

> But blessed are those who trust in the LORD
> and have made the LORD their hope and confidence.
> They are like trees planted along a riverbank,
> with roots that reach deep into the water.
> Such trees are not bothered by the heat
> or worried by long months of drought.
> Their leaves stay green,
> and they never stop producing fruit.[4]

Jeremiah contrasts stunted shrubs with an image of a firmly planted tree, producing fruit even in the harshest of droughts. The conditions are the same, as both the stunted shrubs and fruit trees experience droughts and heat. The difference, Jeremiah tells us, is roots that connect to Life. It's making the Lord, not ourselves, our source of hope: turning upward, not inward.

This theme emerged consistently in our conversations with global leaders. We did not hear about self-reliance; we heard about faith. We did not hear about strength and resolve; we heard about roots.

Ultimately, where our roots find their source of life makes the difference between a fruit-bearing tree and a brittle shrub. This is the difference Jeremiah calls out. It's not about our own strength. It's not about a new model of self-help. Rather, it's about deep trust, connection, and reliance on God—despite harsh, even brutal, conditions.

Similarly, Jesus tells us the way to produce fruit—and speaks frankly of our limitations—in John 15: "A branch cannot produce fruit if it is severed from the vine, and you cannot be fruitful unless you remain in me. . . . Those who remain in me, and I in them, will produce much fruit. For apart from me you can do nothing."[5]

Jesus tells us that when we are connected to the Source of Life, there is fresh fruit. On our own, we become barren and stunted.

We've asserted in the preceding chapters that disillusionment is a gift. That's because disillusionment shatters the illusion—the idol—of self-sufficiency. This is when God reminds us that He has been there all along, inviting us to look not inward—to our finite abilities—but upward. As Kyle Idleman argues in *Don't Give Up*, "The point of defeat . . . seems like the most desolate corner of creation. [But] it actually places you in prime position to experience God's strength and provision because, as it turns out, God is drawn to the desperate."[6] And the desperate are drawn to God.

The Idol of Grit

In our own leadership journey, we feel the seductive pull of turning inward. We strive to be and appear *anything but* desperate.

We began this book heavily influenced by our reading on grit and resilience. While we have benefited from and enthusiastically endorse books such as *Grit* by Angela Duckworth and *The Resilience Factor* by Karen Reivich and Andrew Shatte, as we researched and wrote, we recognized our own temptation to embrace our culture's obsession with self-improvement. To place our trust in our own abilities, grit, and resilience. To elevate these virtues in the global leaders we profile. Yet we began to recognize that they make a faulty foundation for sustaining our service.

Grit and resilience are rightly recognized and celebrated. The leaders we profile exude these traits, but they spoke of them not as the secret source of their long-term service but as the manifestation of something deeper.

In her book *Can't Even: How Millennials Became the Burnout Generation*, journalist Anne Peterson describes our society's addiction to easy fixes to the hopelessness we feel.

> We gravitate toward these personal cures because they seem tenable, and promise that our lives can be recentered, and regrounded, with just a bit more discipline, a new app, a better email organization strategy, or

Grit and resilience are rightly recognized and celebrated—but as the manifestation of something deeper.

a new approach to meal planning. But these are merely Band-Aids on an open wound. They might temporarily stop the bleeding, but when they fall off, and we fail at our new-found discipline, we just feel worse.[7]

While Anne Peterson may not agree with Jeremiah's prescription, she identifies just how insufficient these strategies are in creating the change they promise. Jeremiah and the global leaders led us to a conclusion that is far simpler and far more profound than we anticipated: Grit and resilience flow from our rootedness in the God of hope. They are the fruit, not the root.

The leaders we interviewed emphasized Holy Spirit encounters, commitments and callings, and how Jesus held them in their moments of greatest crisis. They spoke of turning upward and outward, not inward.

God invites us to be people who look up. Who remember that we have nowhere else to go. As we read in Psalm 121, "I look up to the mountains—does my help come from there? My help comes from the LORD, who made heaven and earth!"⁸ Or as the author of Hebrews invites us, "Let us run with endurance the race God has set before us. We do this by keeping our eyes on Jesus, the champion who initiates and perfects our faith."⁹

This approach is dramatically different from the self-help formulas dominating our podcasts, bookshelves, and culture. It's reaching the end of our own strength and turning to the God who invites us into holy surrender. It's not a neat and tidy list of five steps to bulletproof our ministry or organization; it's far more radical, though perhaps simpler as well. It's an invitation to turn to God and away from the idolization of our own abilities.

We see this decision to look upward in global leaders who endure exile, grow through suffering, surrender their own agendas, and commit to their calling despite entrenched conflict. They are following the example set thousands of years ago through the faithful obedience of the prophet Jeremiah, and as a result, they experience fruit even in times of drought.

Application Questions

1. When has attempting to live by your own strength let you down?
2. What good things have you elevated to the point of idolatry?
3. What do you think when you read Jesus' words in John 15, "Apart from me you can do nothing"?
4. What would it mean for you to turn upward rather than inward?

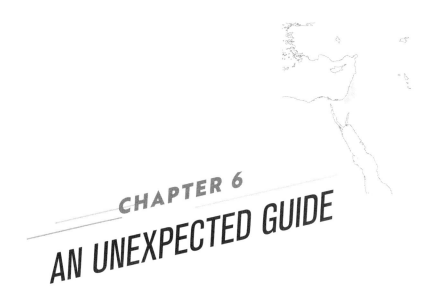

CHAPTER 6

AN UNEXPECTED GUIDE

I knew you before I formed you in your mother's womb. Before you were born I set you apart and appointed you as my prophet to the nations.

—Jeremiah 1:5

We didn't expect to unearth insights into enduring hope in a book often considered a primer on despair, written by a man nicknamed "The Weeping Prophet." But in every interview we conducted, the words Jeremiah spoke or the themes he addressed came up with almost uncanny consistency. We needed to learn more about this Old Testament prophet and the context in which he delivered such timeless wisdom. What does Jeremiah, a man most closely associated with lament, have to teach us about enduring hope?

Jeremiah was called to prophetic ministry in 626 BC before he was even twenty years old. At the moment of Jeremiah's commissioning, God gives him a prophetic message of judgment and rebuilding[1] and warns that his message will be fiercely opposed by his own people. Yet it is precisely this call that will carry Jeremiah through.

"Out of that commission of Jeremiah comes his resilient hope," writes theologian Walter Brueggemann.[2]

For the next forty years, through the reign of multiple monarchs in the kingdom of Judah, Jeremiah delivers prophetic words to a nation in decline. At God's command, Jeremiah denounces the nation's wickedness and its failure to respond to God's call. The prophet experienced disillusionment as leaders consistently ignored his calls to repentance.

He faced death threats, assaults, imprisonment, slander, and abduction.[3] Yet, in stark contrast to the nation of Judah, he remained faithful to God and His call. As one commentary summarizes, "One of the striking things about Jeremiah was his tenacious faithfulness in carrying out God's instructions in the face of unrelenting opposition and harsh criticism."[4]

Perhaps he would be more aptly called The Persevering Prophet.[5]

Though he persevered, Jeremiah at times protested and struggled with God. He calls out to God and says, "You misled me."[6] He claims that God wasn't honest about how difficult this call was going to be. He is deeply disillusioned. "Jeremiah perseveres in hope," writes Old Testament scholar Samuel Hildebrandt, "but he also struggles and despairs of the calling that he's received. I always found it deeply liberating and hopeful that perseverance can look so frail, so honest."[7]

Despite struggles and pain, Jeremiah could be faithful because God had promised to be faithful to him. He served with trust in God's promise: "They will fight you, but they will fail. For I am with you, and I will take care of you."[8]

Israel and Judah were living in the Promised Land, yet having reached this destination, they failed to pursue the God who led them there and instead chased after idols and geopolitical allies.[9] Early in Jeremiah's ministry, God tells him, "For my people have done two evil things: they have abandoned me—the fountain of living water. And they have dug for themselves cracked cisterns that can hold no water at all!"[10]

"Water—living non-stagnant water—is essential for life in a desert land like Israel," writes Old Testament scholar Kathleen O'Connor. "To preserve it, people dug cisterns, but suicidal Israel abandons life-sustaining water for leaky, useless holes in the ground, that is, the [false gods known as] ba'als."[11]

Metaphorically speaking, they traded streams of living water for the stagnant water found in the leaky pits of their own creation. They ceased looking upward and turned to the illusion of self-reliance, looking inward to what they could provide for themselves, depending on their own strength and resourcefulness rather than on God's faithful provision and protection.

Perhaps those most in need of a reminder of the insufficiency of self-sufficiency were Judah's leaders. The book of Jeremiah is full of particularly harsh words for corrupt religious and political leaders who use their position for personal gain.[12]

Jeremiah had a seemingly impossible task: communicate a message from God to a people who most certainly did not want to listen. Empowered with words not his own,[13] Jeremiah spoke out against the greed of priests and the foolishness of false prophets. He spoke truth to religious and political powers who had ignored God.[14] In every instance, he challenged the powerful to return to God and reject the temptation to trust in themselves.

Jeremiah expected—and endured—repercussions for speaking out against the ruling powers. For his message, religious leaders beat Jeremiah and put him in stocks at the Upper Gate of Benjamin, humiliating him with mockery and public abuse. The words he spoke offended the religious elite and those who believed Judah was invincible. Their confidence was in their nation, religious institutions, and the kings who governed. These leaders were infected with the "disease of autonomy," believing in their own strength and sufficiency alone.[15]

A group of influential priests tried to convince King Zedekiah to put Jeremiah to death, eventually settling on the indirect method of throwing Jeremiah into deep mud at the bottom of a cistern, where it was assumed he would starve.[16]

As if that were not enough, Jeremiah was not exempt from the judgment his people faced. Eventually, as Jeremiah prophesied, the Babylonians invaded Judah, and the nation fell into captivity in 586 BC under the ruthless rule of King Nebuchadnezzar. Jeremiah continues writing as the kingdom begins to implode and his dire predictions of judgment begin to materialize.

Jeremiah delivered the message that his people would experience captivity, displacement, and exile for seventy years: almost two full generations. Throughout Jeremiah, there is a lot of bad news. Destruction. Judgment. Pain.

"We may wonder what it does to [Jeremiah]. It could drive him to denial, to cynicism, to assimilation; but it does not," writes Brueggemann.[17] "It will be Jeremiah who is the voice of suffered hope."

It takes work to trudge through the bad news until you eventually reach the good news. But the good news is so very good. In the midst of overwhelming pain, God says, in Jeremiah 29:11, in a letter Jeremiah penned to the exiles, there is a hope and a future. Throughout Jeremiah, we see these glimmers of hope. God promises He will restore and renew all that they see destroyed around them.[18] It is a message grounded not in current circumstances but in God's unchanging mercy and graciousness. Restoration will come, but for Jeremiah and sometimes for us, it does not come quickly. Rarely does it come on our terms or within our timelines.

To encourage those who heard his words to hold on to hope, Jeremiah extends the timeline of their story. In the wake of a humiliating, soul-crushing defeat from the Babylonians, he reminds the Israelites of God's character and grace. He reminds them of God's promise to be present in the pain and decades of exile. He reminds them that although they were cast out of their homeland, their God still beckons, "Return to Me."

Jeremiah invites the people of Judah to remember their gracious God who gave them a reason to hope even in the rubble.

Living with Hope in Exile

The story of hope while in exile echoes throughout history.

When Adam and Eve ate from the Tree of the Knowledge of Good and Evil, they became the first individuals to place their hope in their own wisdom instead of God's sovereign plan, looking inward rather than upward.[19] They unrealistically believed their own plan would bring them more lasting joy than God's. The serpent's query led to the crossroads of disillusionment, and they questioned whether God's plan really was good. If it wasn't, could they do it better on their own? They would try, and it would lead all of humanity into exile, away from their true home. The reality of cynicism would take root, and humanity would toil for centuries, wondering if positive change and restoration would ever be possible.

Sent away from the comfort, peace, safety, and security of an unblemished relationship with their Creator, Adam and Eve walked into exile, taking all of humanity with them.[20]

Away from our perfect home, we are bound to face trouble. There is a reason Jesus' followers are often called foreigners and exiles.[21] Our hope cannot be found in this world—not in our homes, projects, health, work, or organizations. "These in reality are 'broken cisterns' that look refreshing and promising," writes Samuel Hildebrandt, "but, in the end, will run dry and leave us disappointed."

For some people in the Bible, this exile is clearer than others. Famine causes Israel to live as exiles in Egypt. After 430 years of slavery, they wander 40 years in the wilderness before experiencing 814 years of relative autonomy and security in the Promised Land. But during Jeremiah's ministry, he lives through the complete and final collapse of Israel's failed attempt to live independently of God's provision. When the enemies invade in 586 BC, the symbolic and literal age of Israel's failed experiment of self-reliance comes to a crushing end. The Babylonians destroy the Temple, seen as the residence of God's presence in the Holy City of Jerusalem. The rubble of the sacked Temple is a powerful metaphor and a reminder of Israel's life—and ours—when we insist on holding God at arm's length.

The Assyrians, Babylonians, and Romans all ruled the nation, pushing them again into captivity, slavery, and exile.[22]

Then and now, *we need to learn how to live with hope as people in exile*. How do we hold on to an enduring hope, independent of place or circumstance? In ancient Judah and today, pain and challenge are part of the journey. They are part of living in exile. They are among life's certainties, and no one gets away unscathed.

Perhaps we should return with fresh eyes to the message Jeremiah preached thousands of years ago. We are sojourners in exile, invited to place our unshakable hope not in our own resourcefulness or resilience but in the One who leads us home. We remember the One who has

> ## We are invited to reside not in a location but in a relationship.

called us, beckoning us to live here on earth "as it is in heaven."[23] We are invited to reside not in a location but in a relationship.

Hebrews 13:14 says, "For this world is not our permanent home; we are looking forward to a home yet to come." This side of eternity, harsh conditions exist. Challenges are real, but there is hope—even knee-deep in the mud of a cistern, in the stocks, or under siege. Even as we long for home, there is hope.

Unshakable Hope

The advice we offer each other—*Don't give up; don't give in; don't lose hope*—is woefully insufficient.

It's like looking at a tree and shouting, "Grow apples!"

No matter how enthusiastically or exuberantly we shout, the fruit isn't going to appear. Fruit appears because years earlier a seed was planted and covered by healthy soil. A taproot shot down, and a sapling grew up. Then with sun, rain, and patience, the plant grew.

The fruit is easy to see and delicious to taste, but what's often missed is all that has been happening beneath the surface for years. Without the root, there can be no fruit. Jeremiah's message from God bears repeating:

> "Blessed are those who trust in the LORD
> and have made the LORD their hope and confidence.
> They are like trees planted along a riverbank,
> with roots that reach deep into the water.
> Such trees are not bothered by the heat
> or worried by long months of drought.

Their leaves stay green,
　　and they never stop producing fruit."[24]

Jeremiah instructs us that leaders' enduring hopefulness grows out of their deep connection to the God they serve. We see the fruit of their faithful service but need to dig deeper to understand what has nourished that fruit. There are certainly behaviors to emulate, but ultimately there's a connection to deepen. The message in Jeremiah is a call for people to stop idolizing their own strength and acknowledge absolute dependence on the Creator.[25]

This is the difference of enduring hopefulness. It's not humanism, and it's not idealism. It's not a *go get 'em, try harder* inspirational message. It's not checklists and practices to get grittier. It's not a five-step process to develop more resilience.

Rather, it's a connection to the Spring of living water,[26] the Author of life, and the Restorer of the broken. Unshakable hope is grounded in a bigger story. It's informed optimism, not blind idealism, because it's connected to the character of God, who remains faithful in seasons of drought as well as seasons of plenty.

Idols are worthless; they are ridiculous lies!
　　On the day of reckoning they will all be destroyed.
But the God of Israel is no idol!
　　He is the Creator of everything that exists.[27]

We haven't yet reached that long-awaited ending, and brokenness surrounds us. For the exiles Jeremiah writes to, there is also a promised ending—yet for this generation, Babylon would be their home. They weren't only called to serve their time and suffer their consequences. They were called to actively "work for the peace and prosperity of the city where I sent you into exile. Pray to the LORD for it."[28]

Similarly, we aren't meant to just lament the brokenness of this world while we passively await rescue. God invites us to engage. To get to work. To heal and to hope.

The Quest

There is a journey from idealism to enduring hope. As with any journey, there are opportunities to veer off course. But there is always God's invitation, issued by Jeremiah to the people of Judah long ago and to us today: Return to Me. Stop looking inward at your strength and resolve. Look up.

> Can any of the worthless foreign gods send us rain?
>   Does it fall from the sky by itself?
> No, you are the one, O Lord our God!
>   Only you can do such things.
>   So we will wait for you to help us.[29]

We cannot do this in our own strength. We need to discover God's presence that alone leads to an enduring hope. Based on our exploration of Jeremiah and other leaders who exemplify an enduring hope, the next four stories highlight four defining characteristics of leaders who look up:

- They identify the only certain place to root their hope (chapter 7).
- They anticipate pain and view suffering as an invitation to draw near (chapter 8).
- They surrender their strengths (chapter 9).
- They have a clear calling and commitment: a beautiful obligation (chapter 10).

Application Questions

1. Where have you seen evidence of God's unchanging mercy and graciousness?
2. How does the concept of "exile" apply to your own life?
3. Unshakable hope is grounded in a bigger story. How does this bigger story impact the way you live and lead?

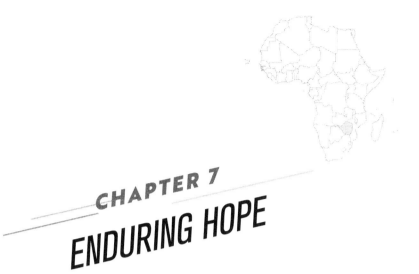

CHAPTER 7
ENDURING HOPE

Hope acts on the conviction that God will complete the work that he has begun even when the appearances, especially when the appearances, oppose it.

—Eugene Peterson[1]

Sometimes the journey isn't the one we anticipated. Farai Mutamiri never imagined himself in a position of church leadership, though today he is the bishop of the Anglican Diocese of Harare, Zimbabwe. "This was never my dream," he laughs. And that was before he knew of the violence and death threats that would accompany the role.

Farai was born in 1968, twelve years before Zimbabwe gained independence from Britain. He grew up in a time of postcolonial possibility, the country buoyed by optimism over the promise and potential of self-governance, even amid continued hardship. Three of Farai's nine siblings died from preventable diseases, and his own family's struggle was just one indicator of the ongoing impact of poverty and the challenges his nation still faced post-independence.

Farai excelled academically and, after graduating from college, found employment in the private sector. On weekends, he volunteered with the Anglican church he attended, and it didn't take long before church leaders noticed his volunteer service and invited him to consider joining the church in a full-time capacity.

Surprised by the invitation, he took time to pray and seek God's will. "I wondered, is this what God called me to?" Though he asked for a sign, Farai heard nothing. "I didn't see any sign. I didn't feel anything. And so, I didn't move forward in exploring a role with the church." Wanting to avoid an awkward conversation with the rector who had proposed the idea, Farai began arriving at church late and leaving early. Eventually, the rector stopped him, and Farai confessed, "I've been trying to search for answers to this calling, but I never got one."

The rector's response was profound in its simplicity: "Let us continue to pray."

They both continued to pray, and two years later, Farai felt God's prompting and peace about this life-altering decision. He officially joined the Anglican Church with hope, envisioning his church engaged in service and positively impacting the nation. He had taken time and space to consider this calling and was prepared to serve, love, and lead. He imagined a unified church, standing in solidarity in Zimbabwe and with the global Christian community.

Full of optimism, Farai imagined what might be possible through an engaged Church in Zimbabwe. Much like Jo Anne, he spoke of his early vision of "justice [rolling] down like waters, and righteousness like an ever-flowing stream."[2] He believed hearts would turn to God, hope would be unleashed, and lives would be changed.

As we've already discussed, disillusionment is inevitable for the idealist. For Farai, he never imagined it would arrive so quickly.

Misplaced Optimism

When Farai was young, he memorized a Bible verse that tops the charts year after year. It's among the most quoted, most searched, and most memed.[3] It's Jeremiah 29:11, where God promises a prosperous hope and future: "'For I know the plans I have for you,' declares the LORD, 'plans to prosper you and not to harm you, plans to give you hope and a future'" (NIV).

This verse from Jeremiah might be among the most popular, but—often removed from its original context as a letter written to a people suffering forceful displacement and exile in a foreign, hostile environment—it's also arguably one of the most misinterpreted verses in Scripture.

Disconnected from its original circumstances, plucked out of context, and planted in cheery memes, Jeremiah 29:11 is trivialized as a blanket promise for prosperity and blessing. Out of context, this verse not only perpetuates but also fuels the *false hope* of idealism, taking its place alongside an ostrich with its head in the sand, the pie in the sky, and unicorns jumping over rainbows. The verse has been used as a broad assurance for things to always get better. For prosperity to come and harm to stay far away.

Inevitably, we discover things do not always get better. Progress often happens at a snail's pace and follows a winding course. The great irony of Jeremiah 29:11 is that it was written in the days following the first major attack by Babylon on Judah in 597 BC.[4] This was a moment when the people were left without leadership, when the looming threat of Babylon had become a cruel reality, when the occupying force had won, when hope was lost. After generations of independence and autonomy, this first attack on Judah marked the beginning of the end of everything in which God's people had placed their confidence.

But the hope Jeremiah wrote of was not rooted in Judah's circumstances, which were bleak at best. It was not an idealistic hope but a hope that holds—even in moments of pain and destruction.

Though he memorized Jeremiah 29:11 as a child, Farai came to a very different perspective on this verse and the prophet who penned it as everything he hoped for seemed to be slipping away.

Cloud of Scoundrels

Farai describes Zimbabwe's atmosphere when he became a priest in 1999 as "rosy." But within the next few years, President Robert Mugabe's promises of greater rights and equality in Zimbabwe were growing dim, even as his policies hobbled the economy. In 2003, *The*

Atlantic published an article, "How to Kill a Country: Turning a Bread-basket into a Basket Case in Ten Easy Steps—the Robert Mugabe Way."[5]

Economic crisis fueled corruption in the country, producing deep suffering for most Zimbabweans. Regularly, Farai met with church members who struggled just to put food on the table. No matter how hard people worked, they fell behind as inflation soared. Inflation peaked at an annualized rate of 89.7 sextillion percent, meaning the people of Zimbabwe experienced a daily inflation rate of 98 percent.[6] Prices were essentially doubling every twenty-four hours.

"You feel that pain," Farai shares, echoing the ancient words of Jeremiah, who wrote, "I hurt with the hurt of my people."[7]

"There were moments when I felt helpless," Farai recalls.

Inflation and economic free fall weren't the only concerns. "After independence, our political leaders put the people first, but the longer they stayed in leadership, the more they began putting themselves first," Farai summarizes.

Corruption spread beyond the national government. The senior church leader in Harare, the country's capital, became increasingly aligned with Robert Mugabe's corrupt regime. Church policies blurred with state politics. And when the Church allies with political agendas, the witness of the Church always suffers.

In a bold move, the renegade Anglican leader broke with the broader Church and acquired all Anglican properties (including schools, clinics, and orphanages) in Harare in 2007, with the full support and aggressive backing of Mugabe's police force. Mugabe's loyalists gave church leaders like Farai a terrible choice: align themselves with the corrupt regime or remain locked out of their church buildings and, in some cases, church rectories where they lived. Refusing to align, Farai was evicted from his church and his home.[8]

Unable to worship or meet inside, Anglican priests took their gatherings outdoors. While they could not enter the buildings, they still found ways to worship.

It was at this point, in 2008, that denominational leaders promoted Farai to dean, a more senior leadership role in the Diocese of Harare. The intent was to provide leadership for the people who had refused to follow the renegade bishop and wanted to remain in the province. It was an unenviable position.

"No one wanted the post," Farai laughs. Assuming this role was heralding his opposition both to the politicization of the Church and

> But in Zimbabwe at that time, we were also surrounded by a great cloud of scoundrels.

to the national political leadership. He was standing up and speaking out against injustice, corruption, civil religion, and abuse of power.

Farai exudes warmth and humor, even when reflecting on the pain of this time. "Hebrews 12 shares that we are surrounded by a great cloud of witnesses. But in Zimbabwe at that time, we were also surrounded by a great cloud of scoundrels."

When leaders voiced criticism against President Mugabe or church leaders, or took a stand counter to government or church policy, their lives were in danger. Farai did both frequently in his mission to serve God and the Church faithfully.

Jail Cells and Tear Gas

On multiple occasions, the police arrested Farai for holding Sunday services. "I would spend nights in a lice-infested cell just because I had conducted a service," he says.

When Farai felt God calling him to ministry, this was not what he thought he was signing up for. By this point, idealism had long since ceded to disillusionment over the extent of corruption of the national government and church leadership. And the challenges only escalated.

"I would get death threats," Farai shares. "My family was victimized. My kids were victimized. It was tough, but I believed in the mission, and I knew we were standing up for what was right."

Farai could have given in to fear, despair, self-pity, or cynicism. Or he could have dug deeper for the resolve to make it through one more week . . . one more confrontation . . . one more threat . . . in his own strength. But instead, he turned upward. "Though we were under pressure, I knew in my heart that I was serving a living God."

Farai did not place his hope in his own ability to restore his community, church, and country. Farai knew that true, enduring hope is not a promise that everything will work out exactly the way we would have it. Rather, it is surrendering and placing our hope in God alone.

Enduring hope: *our complete trust and active expectation in God's redemptive work.*

Connecting his experience to that of the early Church encouraged Farai. He was hardly the first believer thrown in jail.

"We felt like we were reliving the persecution of the early Church, and I was proud to have been associated with the suffering of the faithful followers." Farai was not interested in settling for a hope that only brought false comfort. Instead, he placed his hope in the conviction that God is making all things new, trusting that He serves as our Comforter in the meantime.

The threats persisted, as did Farai's willingness to stand against corruption—anchored in his scriptural understanding of who the Church is called to be and his faith in a living God. One night at eleven o'clock, two men claiming to be government agents arrived at his home, banging on the gate. Farai eventually opened it and met armed officials, who delivered an unmistakably clear threat: "Your days are numbered. You will die."

At that moment, Farai recalls that he felt filled with the Holy Spirit. He replied, echoing the words of the apostle Paul, "My life is not my own. I am not afraid of death. One day I will meet my Maker. And until then, I will remain faithful."[9]

As he closed the gate, shivers raced through his body, and he collapsed. Farai knows that he could not have mustered the strength to stand and face this threat alone. As Acts 1:8 promises, "You will receive power when the Holy Spirit comes on you; and you will be my witnesses in Jerusalem, and in all Judea and Samaria, and to the ends of the earth" (NIV).

The threats continued, but Farai's resolve only strengthened. His congregation referred to this time as their exile period, and Farai routinely preached from the book of Jeremiah. When God spoke through Jeremiah, "all of His words would over time become the anchor, the script of meaning-making, and the source of hope in Israel's time of exile." The fall of Jerusalem is acknowledged at the start of the book and addressed in its final chapter, "thus framing the entire book as a message to exiles"[10]—which applied to the people of God experiencing exile both in Babylon and in Zimbabwe.

"The words of Jeremiah burst alive in the midst of cataclysms and extreme suffering today," writes theologian Kathleen O'Connor. "It is into this abyss that the book of Jeremiah accompanies victims, as if with a lantern to light the way."[11]

As Farai continued to preach, the police would predictably descend and arrest him. They hoped to instill fear in the congregation, but the authorities didn't anticipate the outcome of their actions. Persecution strengthened the church.

Francis Kaitano, country director of HOPE Zimbabwe, recalls how the words of a nineteenth-century Anglican hymn became the congregants' rallying cry: "Christian, seek not yet repose, Cast thy dreams of ease away; Thou art in the midst of foes: Watch and pray."

Farai remembers, "We became so strong. People would come to church with their Bibles and with wet towels, so they were prepared for tear gas. You'd wonder where we were getting that zeal and energy."

They remained faithful—watching, praying, and casting aside any dreams of ease—even as they faced continued abuse, discouragement from unjust court decisions and self-serving church leaders, and the silence of other faith communities.

"We saw injustice of all kinds," Farai recalls. Yet he also remembers how the Anglican congregations held on to hope and began to intentionally seek what God might be teaching them. They let go of the physical buildings and discovered that the Church was never about stone and bricks. "Perhaps we were too attached to our buildings and not attached enough to God."

Farai believes that, though harrowing, this persecution refined the Church. "When people are used to a certain type of worship and church experience, it can become routine. You don't put your mind to what you're doing." Suffering and the end of idealism brought clarity, renewal, and resolve.

"We had become too comfortable," Farai shares. "This was a way of waking us up, revitalizing our faith and revitalizing our hope."

Realizing that the church building is only a temporary structure, they got to work loving each other and standing together against the corruption of the Church and national government. "Sometimes, you need to be out of the church building to realize how important God is in your life."

Farai also preached messages of hope—messages that, even in exile, God is with them. There is still a hope and a future. Amid much suffering in Zimbabwe, the gospel advanced.

Eventually, in November 2012, the Zimbabwean Supreme Court ruled that Anglican congregations could move back into their church buildings. The exile was over, and the rebuilding process began. While the physical buildings had fallen into disrepair during these five years of exile, the believers' faith and sense of community had grown stronger.

The challenges shattered Farai's idealism about church service, yet God used this pain to deepen faith, resilience, and commitment: signs that He was at work through this crisis. With the gift of hindsight, Farai concludes, "These challenges helped us know who we are and our purpose in life."

Revisiting Jeremiah

Throughout the most challenging seasons in Zimbabwe, Farai returned to Jeremiah and the verse he had memorized as a child. As he preached messages from this Old Testament prophet, he discovered they were full of modern-day relevance. Jeremiah's prescription for hope became relevant for Farai and those who sought to faithfully follow God in Zimbabwe.

The temptation to draw our hope from the wrong sources threatened Farai and threatens us. We are misguided when we place our confidence in our circumstances and our success. When our hope is contingent on our abilities or when we assess our message based on the response it receives. We "trust in mere humans, who rely on human strength and turn their hearts away from the LORD."[12]

Despite tear gas and death threats, Farai and his congregation chose to believe and cling to the promise of Jeremiah 29:11, regardless of the bleak circumstances around them. Their hope was rooted not in their circumstances, nor in their ability to change them, but in a deep-seated trust in God's infinite faithfulness.

This path to true and enduring hope brought courage in the face of persecution—the ability to stand firm in fear. Both then and now, enduring hope grows in suffering as we learn to trust God and His redemptive plan for our lives and contexts. When all seemed to be lost for Jeremiah and for Israel, when God "takes away what is treasured but has become unacceptable," He makes a "new form of life possible in the world, just when all seemed ended and beyond recall."[13]

Ezekiel, the priest and contemporary to Jeremiah who lived through this tumultuous season of Babylon's conquest of Jerusalem, joined Jeremiah in mourning the death of Israel's failed attempt at autonomy. But he does not stop there. Like Jeremiah, he too communicates bright hope for what is to come. In a familiar and powerful metaphor, Ezekiel paints the hopeful picture of life emerging from decay. Of skeletons returning to life.

"These bones represent the people of Israel," God says to Ezekiel. "They are saying, 'We have become old, dry bones—all hope is gone. Our nation is finished.'"[14]

But from death and lost hope, life emerges. "Look! I am going to put breath into you and make you live again!" God promises Israel. "I will put flesh and muscles on you and cover you with skin. I will put breath into you, and you will come to life. Then you will know that I am the LORD."[15]

Brueggemann writes, "Israel is in exile. Israel has been destroyed. Israel has been given the grounds for the judgment of God. Now newness begins to happen. A new shepherd is announced. A new spirit is among the dry bones. A new covenant of peace, a coming out of exile. An experience of new possibility is offered."[16]

God's promise for "a hope and a future" in Jeremiah 29:11 quickly shifts from trite self-help memes to the type of hope transcending even the most difficult circumstances. To the type of hope that produces life from death. It's the same hope that infused Farai when in exile in Zimbabwe and that infuses our service today.

The question remains, what leads us to this type of enduring hope? What helps us look up? The answers are unexpected and uncomfortable—suffering, surrender, and commitment.

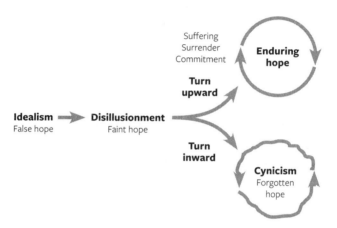

Application Questions

1. In what ways has your journey, like Farai's, been unexpectedly difficult? How have you seen God directing your steps?

2. How have you seen Jeremiah 29:11 and the promise of "a hope and a future" mismatched with its original context?

3. Farai says, "Though we were under pressure, I knew in my heart that I was serving a living God." What difference did that make for Farai, and what difference might it make for you?

4. What does it look like to live with active expectation in God's redemptive work?

CHAPTER 8
SUFFERING

One of the main ways we move from abstract knowledge about God to a personal encounter with him as a living reality is through the furnace of affliction.

—Timothy Keller[1]

With her bright eyes, ready smile, and laugh-lined face, joy seems to emanate from Tita Evertsz. But her light and cheerful countenance belies a story of suffering and redemption.

Over the course of her life, she's faced betrayal from respected Christian leaders, extortion, drug addiction, and domestic abuse. Still, God has brought her from a place of pain to a place where she can look upon deep need and suffering and see nothing but hope.

"I come from a very dark past," Tita shares. "I was definitely a black sheep."

Born in Guatemala to a Christian family, she married young and immigrated to the United States. While she was living in Alhambra, a community near Los Angeles, with her husband and two young children, Tita's life began to fall apart. She and her husband abused cocaine, and her husband also abused her.

When Tita became pregnant with her third child, her husband pressured her to abort the baby. It was in this valley that Tita describes crying out to God for help.

"I lit a candle and asked God to please help me," she recalls.

At Tita's rock bottom, God reminded her that she still had a choice. She had chosen to run her life as she saw fit, but now she could choose to surrender to Him. That day, from a place of utter despair, Tita made the decision that has guided every choice since: submitting her life to Jesus. For the first time, she recognized the insufficiency of turning inward and looked upward.

Tita abandoned a life of drugs, fled her abusive husband, and returned to Guatemala with her children, eager to serve the God who had saved her.

As Tita began to rebuild her life, every impulse should have been to pursue a life of safety, stability, and security for herself and her children. But God began to nurture within her a passion to serve people experiencing the very sort of pain she had escaped. She had Good News, and God drew her to communities of pain and brokenness, where people needed it desperately.

That was perhaps nowhere truer than in a nearby slum called *La Limonada*. The name literally translates "The Lemonade." Once a verdant ravine where lemon trees grew so thick their essence lingered in the air, La Limonada became inhabited by internally displaced Guatemalans fleeing for their lives after the overthrow of the country's president in 1954.[2]

In the more than three decades of civil war that followed, La Limonada's population continued to grow. With no urban planning or infrastructure, La Limonada grew to become the largest urban slum in Central America: one of the poorest communities in one of the poorest countries in the world.[3] With more than 60,000 people, it was dirty, and it was dangerous. Residents of nearby Guatemala City neighborhoods say, "Not even Santa Claus goes to La Limonada."[4]

But Tita went there. "What I saw was people in great need, in deep darkness like I was in before," Tita reflects. "In my heart, I just wanted to share, 'There is a way out! There is hope!' I needed to share Jesus

Christ with them." She had tasted the Living Water and wanted to point others to the Source.

Tita began ministering to children in the hospital. While there, she met a gang member in the intensive care unit and ministered to him as well. Soon she was reaching beyond the hospital to gang members, drug dealers, and prostitutes in the "red zone" community that Guatemalan journalist José Alejandro Adamuz Hortelano referred to as "a cemetery"—for the living.[5]

The longer she served in La Limonada, the more committed she became to its people and their flourishing.

As Tita began to build friendships within this community, she invited her new friends to join her at her church, which was located in a wealthier community. At first, things went well. But over time, church leaders grew uncomfortable with Tita's new friends.

"The pastor told me, 'Your people are making my people leave the church.'"

The pastor told Tita her friends were not welcome there. Broken over the church's rejection of the hurting, Tita grieved for weeks, deeply disappointed and disillusioned with the church. But then she went with her friends, planting her own church and teaching what she was learning in a Bible study she attended. Alongside the people of La Limonada, Tita worshiped, studied God's Word, praised, and prayed. "It was so beautiful, the church. People were hungry about God and His justice and His Kingdom."

But even in the beauty of her small church, brokenness loomed large. "It has been a great honor to have met the people in deep darkness and see the good and the bright side in them," she reflects. And yet, "It's very painful." One of her regular church attendees, high and insensate, attacked his own wife and ten-year-old daughter with an aerosol can and a lighter. Tita sat with them at the hospital during their painful recovery, walking with them through their suffering.

Tita has witnessed seemingly unceasing tragedy, abuse, and death. She estimates she has seen over a thousand funerals, most of them the result of gang violence.

When we encounter suffering, we may feel God's nearness or we may feel as though God is absent, distant, or disinterested. In Lamentations 5:20, Jeremiah cries out to God, "Why do you continue to forget us? Why have you abandoned us for so long?" But in Jeremiah 12, when the prophet suffers after learning of a plot against his life, he confronts God directly.

> LORD, you always give me justice
>> when I bring a case before you.
> So let me bring you this complaint:
> Why are the wicked so prosperous?
>> Why are evil people so happy?
> You have planted them,
>> and they have taken root and prospered.
> Your name is on their lips,
>> but you are far from their hearts.
> But as for me, LORD, you know my heart.
>> You see me and test my thoughts.
> Drag these people away like sheep to be butchered!
>> Set them aside to be slaughtered![6]

As a direct result of his faithful service, Jeremiah is suffering and persecuted, while those who have forgotten God seem to be flourishing. It isn't right. It isn't fair. He wants relief (and retribution) for his suffering.

God's response is likely not one Jeremiah desired: "If racing against mere men makes you tired, how will you race against horses? If you stumble and fall on open ground, what will you do in the thickets near the Jordan?"[7] In other words, this isn't the worst suffering you may be called to endure.

Then God relates to being forsaken. The people of Jeremiah's hometown have turned on him, and punishment and correction are coming.[8] The people have not just turned on Jeremiah, they have turned away from God. God has become irrelevant to His children. The original Hebrew of the passage captures the pain, calling God's people His "house," His "inheritance," and "the love of [His] life."[9]

"I have abandoned my people, my special possession. I have surrendered my dearest ones to their enemies," God explains to Jeremiah.[10] These people, even in the midst of punishment, are still dearly beloved.

Eugene Peterson aptly notes that in Jeremiah and elsewhere "judgment is not the last word; it is never the last word. . . . Its proper work is to open our hearts to the reality beyond ourselves, to crack the carapace of self-sufficiency so that we can experience the inrushing grace of the healing, merciful, forgiving God."[11]

The goal of judgment is restoration, and the process causes hurt, even to God. "While Yahweh says here that he is abandoning his people,

> ## The goal of judgment is restoration, and the process causes hurt, even to God.

handing them over to their enemies, and destroying them, it is readily apparent that doing so causes him immense pain and suffering," writes scholar David Melvin.[12]

As a result of Judah's unfaithfulness, it isn't just Jeremiah who suffers. God is not detached or distant. God himself suffers. While Jeremiah earned the "weeping prophet" moniker, Old Testament scholar Samuel Hildebrandt says, "Some of the texts that present someone weeping [in the book of Jeremiah] may just as well be assigned to God (e.g., Jeremiah 4:19–21; 8:18–9:3). This in itself is hopeful: God being heartbroken about the condition of his people."

Brokenhearted many times over, Tita gradually felt her optimism giving way to bitterness. But if Tita grieved the injustice and brokenness of La Limonada, how much more must it grieve her heavenly Father? In her prayer times, God guided Tita to Matthew 24:12: "Because of the increase of wickedness, the love of most will grow cold" (NIV).

"I meditated about my love going cold," she shares. "I knew that God is love, and the moment that I walk without love, I'm going to walk without God. So, I repented, prayed for healing, and decided to live by love."

Tita pleaded with God to help her reach people "on time," before they had given their allegiance to gangs, grown addicted to drugs, and lost all hope. And in La Limonada, where gangs recruit minors at an average age of nine, that meant starting young.[13] Over time, Tita sensed God inviting her to invest in the children of La Limonada. In 2000, she started her formal ministry, Vidas Plenas—"Fulfilled Lives"—by launching an academy to serve the children of the community. The academy supplements students' learning, offers nutritious meals and vitamins, teaches hygiene, provides extracurricular activities and Bible studies, and gives children a safe place of belonging.[14]

Seeing Tita's success as a detriment to their recruitment efforts, gangs have threatened and extorted Tita. But she presses on, remembering a meeting several years ago between community leaders and gang members. When a woman asked why the gangs were recruiting children, a gang member responded, "We only pick up the children you are abandoning." Filled with her heavenly Father's love for His children, Tita is not abandoning the children of La Limonada.

Demand for Vidas Plenas's services has continued to grow, so Tita has continued to expand. Today, she operates five schools within La Limonada. Along with her team of fifty-nine educators, psychologists, and social workers, she serves over seven hundred students and their families.

"I can see that we are in a broken world and sin is all over," says Tita. "But God is present. He has called us to be present in this community. In whatever is going on, we are there. We are representing God, light, justice, and hope."

Filled with enduring hope, Tita sees darkness as nothing more than a backdrop against which light can shine.

Expecting Pain

Throughout Scripture, we see that the people who committed their lives to following God experienced immense suffering. It takes willful neglect and massive selectivity to read the Bible and conclude that God's love somehow means we can escape pain.

Jesus himself promises, "In this world you will have trouble."[15] Not among His most inspirational or widely quoted promises, this assurance is one Jesus gives to His closest friends. He is preparing them for what's to come. Speaking plainly, Jesus shares about His impending death and how His followers will be treated afterward. He provides just enough detail for them to be concerned—really concerned.

They will be kicked out of synagogues, treated as outcasts, and hunted by zealots who believe their murderous plots are pleasing to God.[16]

Understandably, His disciples are fearful. This is not what they thought they were signing up for when they accepted Jesus' call to "follow Me." In fact, they likely responded to His initial invitation with a strong dose of idealism for the future: They were following a King they believed was going to overthrow the Roman Empire, and they anticipated seats of honor in the new government. Their excitement likely grew as they saw Jesus heal diseases, alleviate hunger, calm storms, and even raise the dead.

But then, instead of preaching the overthrow of Rome, Jesus prophesied His own death and promised suffering for His disciples, too. Never one to mince words, Jesus affirmed that their journeys would be laced with "trials and sorrows."[17] It would be more agonizing than they could have ever imagined.

Indeed, in the years following Jesus' death, every disciple suffered significantly for their faith, most martyred for their unwavering commitment to Christ.[18] They looked to their Savior, who earned the title of Suffering Servant and "died a criminal's death on a cross" for His "obedience to God."[19] Empowered by the Holy Spirit, these disciples remained faithful and persevered to the very end.

Enduring hope in suffering, modeled for us by Jesus and His disciples, is one of the distinctive features of our faith.

Then and now, if we want to follow Christ in this world, we are promised a path that includes pain. It's a path that will inevitably lead to disillusionment as we come to the end of our abilities.

Are we prepared for the journey?

We don't wear sandals to climb Mount Kilimanjaro, and we don't show up to push back darkness without the Light. While there are plenty of surprises in life, we know one thing for sure: This journey will be exceedingly difficult.

We all have firsthand experience and the promise of Jesus to confirm it: "Here on earth you will have many trials and sorrows."[20]

Looking beyond Pain

For Tita and for all of us, suffering is an inevitable part of service. Even though we know suffering produces growth, we rarely welcome it as part of the journey. Pain hurts—literally.

Pain forces us to confront our limits, shattering any illusions of self-sufficiency and beckoning us to turn to God. It strips us of our pride and leads us to the cross, to humility, to an unshakable conviction that we cannot do it on our own. Many have experienced God's nearness when in pain. C. S. Lewis said, "God whispers to us in our pleasures, speaks in our conscience, but shouts in our pain: it is His megaphone to rouse a deaf world."[21]

More than that, pain has the potential to focus our minds and open our hearts. It brings us into closer solidarity with those who are hurting and allows us to spot others' needs more easily. As Charles Spurgeon reflected, "I am certain that I never did grow in grace one-half so much anywhere as I have upon the bed of pain."[22]

We don't want to make suffering sound more noble than it is; it's terrible. Yet we know that while God may not cause suffering, He can use it for our benefit and the benefit of those around us. (Just look at Joseph, Esther, and Jesus.) In fact, God seems to do some of the greatest work in moments of greatest pain. While we never crave suffering, these times often drive us to our knees and to the feet of our Savior.

David Brooks, columnist for the *New York Times*, writes, "When people look forward, when they plan their lives, they say, 'How can I plan . . . [to] make me happy?' . . . But when people look backward at the things that made them who they are, they usually don't talk about moments when they were happy. They usually talk about moments of suffering or healing. So, we plan for happiness, but we're formed by suffering."[23]

In Tita's early years, she saw how God used suffering and met her in her own pain. We can't help but wonder if this gave her more courage or hopefulness as she stepped into La Limonada, a place where she would inevitably encounter even more suffering.

Like Tita, people of enduring hope experience pain yet somehow see beyond it. Each enduringly hopeful leader we interviewed faced setbacks that could have ended their career or even derailed their faith; each one had plenty of opportunities to give up or give in to cynicism. Yet even though they didn't understand all the reasons for their pain, they considered how God might be at work through it. This empowered them to "never stop producing fruit."[24]

In Jeremiah 17, both the stunted shrub and the deep-rooted tree experience heat and drought. For us, too, it's not a question of *if* heat and droughts will come. Instead, the question is, *When* they come, are we connected to Jesus, the Source of Life?

Promised Presence

Immediately after promising troubles to His disciples, Jesus gives us a glimpse of the end of the story: "But take heart, because I have overcome the world."[25]

If we focus only on the first part of Jesus' promise—"Here on earth you will have many trials and sorrows"—we fall into despair. Yet if we focus only on the second part—"I have overcome the world"—we slip into triumphalism or unrealistic idealism. Leaders who endure through suffering are those who hold on to both the pain and the presence.

Moral philosopher John Macmurray lectured on holding in tension the promise of suffering and the promise of presence. "The maxim of illusory religion runs: 'Fear not; trust in God and He will see that none of the things you fear will happen to you'; that of real religion on the contrary is 'Fear not; the things that you are afraid of are quite likely to happen to you, but they are nothing to be afraid of.'"[28]

There are many reasons to despair, but there's an even more compelling reason to cling to hope. It's grounded in a trust not based in our circumstances but in the character of our God. In the first book that bears his name, the apostle Peter writes, "In his kindness God called you to share in his eternal glory by means of Christ Jesus. So after you have suffered a little while, he will restore, support, and strengthen you, and he will place you on a firm foundation."[29] Our suffering may feel longer than "a little while," but Tita knows these are the moments to keep looking up to the God who is with us in our pain.

Application Questions

1. How have you been "formed by suffering"?

2. When you experience suffering, what do you tend to believe about God? Do you believe He is near or distant, present or disinterested?

3. What would change if you believed God is present and heart-broken in our suffering with us as His dearly beloved?

4. What would it look like to embrace suffering in our lives with enduring hope as Jesus modeled for us?

5. How can we use our own suffering to better serve those who are hurting and in need?

CHAPTER 9

SURRENDER

No amount of determination will bring freedom. We're going to learn to
be victorious by surrendering our lives completely to the Spirit of God,
not by gritting our teeth and trying harder.

—Beth Moore[1]

There was no one that Taysir (Tass) Saada hated more than the Jewish people.

Born in Gaza, Tass grew up against a backdrop of bitter enmity
between the Israeli and Palestinian people, who both laid claim to the
same territory.

Just three years before Tass's birth, his parents, originally from Jaffa,
had uprooted their lives and fled forty miles away to the Palestinian territory of Gaza during the Arab–Israeli War of 1948. They hoped and
planned to return to their homeland after the war.

Despite having a larger army and better artillery, however, the Arabs
lost the war to Israel in 1948, resulting in the creation of Israel as the
Jewish state and the forced emigration of up to 750,000 Palestinians.[2]

Realizing they would not be able to return to their home in Jaffa, Tass's
parents moved the entire family from Gaza to Saudi Arabia to Qatar to
live as Palestinian emigrants. Their frequent moves took an emotional and

physical toll, leaving young Tass deeply ashamed. Tass recounts a Palestinian saying that summarized his feelings at the time: "A man without land is a man without honor, and a man without honor is better dead."

From an early age, Tass developed a deep-seated hatred for the Jewish people—a hatred birthed from losing his homeland and living in disgrace as an emigrant. He looked for a leader who would restore his family's dignity and bring the Palestinians back to their homeland. And he believed he found that leader in Yasser Arafat, the chairman of the Palestine Liberation Organization (PLO). When Arafat came to visit Qatar, Tass's father, a donor to his cause, hosted Arafat in their home. Tass, a young teenager at the time, admired Arafat's bold, brash leadership and his commitment to the Palestinian people.

In 1967, war broke out again. This time, Israel took up arms against neighboring Egypt, Syria, and Jordan. Incredibly, in just six days, Israel defeated the Arab forces and seized the West Bank and East Jerusalem.

Tass had grown increasingly incensed against Israel, and their victory was the last straw. He couldn't understand why the Arabs—who were larger in size and artillery—continued to lose wars to Israel. Determined to fight for his land, he approached his father about joining Fatah, an underground network that advocated armed resistance against Israel.

His father adamantly refused, telling Tass he needed to focus on his studies instead. Defiant, Tass forged his father's signature on the application and ran away from home at seventeen. He joined Fatah, the largest faction of the PLO, in Jordan in the late 1960s under the leadership of his hero, Yasser Arafat.

With Arafat's endorsement, Tass became a commander of units. He and his team underwent intense training, which included drills such as escaping a speeding car and jumping from a five-story building.

Known for his blazing anger toward Israel and his hatred of the Jews, Tass was considered a noteworthy fighter and swiftly rose through the ranks, even becoming a personal driver for Arafat. By the time he was in his late teens, Tass had been trained as an assassin. While his peers back home were studying history and mathematics, he was learning about explosives and martial arts.

Trained to kill, Tass earned the nickname "The Butcher." His job was to study and kill Israeli soldiers, particularly commanders of units.

After four years of serving with Fatah, he simply couldn't kill anymore. Burdened by the brutality of his work, he left the movement at age twenty-one. Arafat told him, "Young man, you're a natural-born leader. You can do better for our cause if you get an education and fight with your brain instead of your weapon."

Starting Over

Tass followed Arafat's urging, and in 1974 he moved to the United States to study at the University of Missouri. He was convinced he'd hate America—which his father eloquently referred to as "the country of the great Satan"—primarily because of its unflagging support of Israel.

But the warm welcome Tass received surprised him. "As a Palestinian, it made me happy that [Americans] did not see me as an immigrant or a refugee," he recollects. The kindness and acceptance caught him off guard, especially as he remembered how poorly he and his family had been treated as refugees in the Middle East. Eventually, he met and married an American woman, Karen, and obtained a green card to stay in America.

He found work as a busser in a small French restaurant in Kansas City. Coming from an affluent Middle Eastern family, Tass found it shameful to work in the restaurant industry. After accepting the job, he grew increasingly anxious, wanting to ensure that no one back home would ever find out. On his first day bussing tables, he was so nervous that his hands shook visibly. Charlie Sharp, a businessman whom Tass had never seen before, was sitting at a table Tass cleared. "Thank you, young man," he said to Tass with a smile. Tass was taken aback. The man not only acknowledged him but *thanked* him? Where he came from, they never thanked the servers.

Those four words started a lifelong friendship. Tass served Charlie every time he came into the restaurant. "I wasn't looking for Christ or Christianity at all," Tass shares. "But God used that *thank you* to begin a relationship."

A Saul-to-Paul Transformation

Over the next nineteen years, Tass worked his way up from busboy to the owner of a drive-through restaurant, and Tass's relationship with Charlie grew stronger. The defining moment of their friendship came on March 14, 1993.

That morning, Tass was experiencing massive panic attacks stemming from the trauma of his past. Tass remembered that Charlie once told him he had "connections" and pointed to heaven. Desperate to know what these connections were, Tass called Charlie. Afraid to leave Tass alone, Charlie picked him up and drove him back to his house. Then, in a soft but firm voice, Charlie began, "Tass, if you want to experience peace, you have to love the Jews."

Charlie had shared a few of his "absurd Christian ideas" over the years, but this was by far the most repugnant. Love the *Jews*? The people who had taken his homeland, forced him from his country, terrorized his friends and neighbors, and stripped him and his family of all sense of peace and security?

Tass had heard enough. He jumped out of his chair in a rage. "What's wrong with you?" he screamed at Charlie. "That's blasphemy!" Tass's fury grew as Charlie tried to calm him down.

Charlie began reading from the book of John, "'In the beginning was the Word, and the Word was with God, and the Word was God.'"[3] This was as far as Charlie got when Tass began to shake violently and then passed out. When Tass regained consciousness, he found himself on his knees with his arms lifted in the air, inviting Jesus to be his Lord and Savior.

A few seconds later, a brilliant Light burst into the room. Just as had happened two thousand years earlier to another murderer on the road to Damascus, Tass immediately fell back. He heard, "I am Jesus. I am the Way, the Truth, and the Life. There is no way to the Father except through Me."

Tass could hardly move. In an instant, Jesus had become undeniably real. With Charlie by his side, he surrendered his life to Christ.[4]

Radically transformed, in the weeks that followed, Tass studied the Scriptures. Reading through the Old Testament was painstaking for the first two years after his conversion. "I loved Jesus but wanted to find a way to follow without having to love the Jews."

The New Testament didn't provide an easy solution either. In Matthew 5:43–44, Tass read, "You have heard the law that says, 'Love your neighbor' and hate your enemy. But I say, love your enemies! Pray for those who persecute you!"

He leapt from his chair. "No way, God. I'll never love them." He started sobbing as he listed for God all the reasons why he wouldn't—couldn't—love the Jewish people. "They stole my homeland and my livelihood. They took everything from me!"

"They have done more than that to me," he heard God reply. "But I still love them."

Tass's perspective began to shift as he looked upward. Through tears, he responded, "If You love them, then I will love them, too. But You need to help me. I cannot do it on my own."

God of Second Chances

Tass didn't notice a change until a few weeks later as he prepared to buy a building from a Jewish landlord. "When I met with Jewish businesspeople," Tass says, "I tried to eat them for lunch before they ate me for dinner." He was determined to be the most aggressive negotiator. But as he spent time with the man, something felt different. Instead of feeling resentment and hatred, Tass was at peace. His hatred was cleansed by the same Jew he now worshiped.

"When I got to understand God's plan," he shares, "my heart was changed from hating Jews to loving Jews. I was even willing to die for the soul of a Jew. That's how much God changed my heart. There was no man on earth who could've changed my heart that much." With this newfound love, Tass felt an enormous burden for the years he spent as a trained assassin: "There's nothing that I can do to make up for it."

In December 2000, Tass received a vision from the Lord to drive across America, visiting synagogues to seek forgiveness and visiting mosques to share the gospel. When 9/11 changed the world, an increasing number of churches and mosques invited him to share his unique background and message of reconciliation. Through his story, Tass pointed to a larger story of God's love and redemption for all. His wife, Karen, and his family prayed as he continued this journey.

Tass returned from his trip many months later and, in 2004, founded Hope for Ishmael, "a Christian ministry which seeks to advance Israeli–Palestinian understanding and dialogue as well as to reach Muslims with the gospel of Christ."[5]

Launching an Organization

Four years after God prompted Tass to travel across the United States, Tass again felt God's nudge—this time to bring the gospel to his hometown in the Gaza Strip.

At that time (and still today), Gaza was controlled by Hamas, an Islamist fundamentalist group that most of the world recognizes as a terrorist organization.

"Why Gaza, Lord?" Tass asked. "You know what they'll do to me if they capture me." He hadn't been to Gaza since he was two months old.

Using almost the same words spoken to Jeremiah at the beginning of his call, God spoke again: "Go, for I am with you. Fear not."[6]

In 2005, through a miracle God orchestrated, Tass was able to spend four hours in the Gaza refugee camp where he was born. While there, he heard God's confirmation audibly: "It is time for you to return to your roots." Upon coming home to Missouri, Tass asked his wife to pray about going to live in Gaza. Karen admits she didn't want to go, but when God confirmed to her the truth of Tass's calling, she agreed. They left for the Gaza Strip in May 2006.

The couple's church sent them off well, supporting Hope for Ishmael, while they gained additional support from other churches and organizations. Tass was finally able to bring Hope for Ishmael to the Gaza Strip, creating a cultural center and youth organization.

When the initial launch funds dried up, Tass reached out to places where he had spoken in hopes of partnering with them and receiving their help financially. He remembered churches that eagerly declared they'd stand with him and his team but never followed up with actual support. In the years after he started the ministry in Gaza, just four churches supported the cause.

This season brought a deeper sense of disillusionment with the Church. Not everyone knew how to respond to a believer with a Muslim background, and some reacted with ignorance or apathy. Yet Tass has experienced grace and learned to give it, too. He remained focused on his burden for the Arab–Jewish conflict and his understanding that only Jesus is the answer to it.

"Over twenty years, there have been so many times that I've wanted to throw in the towel, to walk away, and to go back to the business world," Tass says. "Yet God has reminded me that when He gives us the vision, He makes the provision."

"Yes, we get discouraged and disillusioned. Yes, we want to walk away," Tass shares candidly. "But the Spirit of God talks us into staying on, to trust Him, to keep going. We must have that sensitive spirit to hear and fear God when He speaks."

Today, Hope for Ishmael helps families in Gaza with economic development, water wells, and humanitarian aid. It also promotes forgiveness and reconciliation between Arabs and Jews and equips the Christian Church all over the world with the knowledge and resources to reach out to their Muslim neighbors.

Tass considers it his life's mission to work toward reconciliation between the Arabs and the Jews. "Until we are reconciled as Arabs and Jews to the Father," he says, "only then are we reconciled to each other." It's about the work of the cross, and it's Jesus who continues to change hearts. Tass says he's had many Muslims come to him privately and share that they're feeling something different in their hearts toward Jews and wonder if it's normal not to hate them.

Spirit-Filled Transformation

On our own, we don't have what it takes to make this world look like God's Kingdom, nor can we will ourselves to love others with the sacrificial, selfless love Christ has shown us. It's only when God breaks into our lives that we are empowered to love the people we find hardest to love.

This flies in direct contradiction to our culture's messages to try harder, grit it out, or muster up the willpower to forgive. For Tass, and for us, the answer is not more effort. Rather, the answer lies in surrender. Enduring hope flows not from self-help but only from God's help and redemptive power.

In Jeremiah 18, God instructs Jeremiah to visit the potter's house, where an object lesson takes shape. Jeremiah sees the potter diligently laboring at his wheel over a lump of clay, but the clay "did not turn out as he had hoped."[7]

> To give the impression that these are exceptional people would not only be a false rendering of their stories, but it would miss the entire message of the gospel.

Much as we might like to be, we are not the potter in this illustration. We are the lump of clay, serviceable only when yielded to the potter. As Jeremiah watched, the potter began anew, reforming his creation. He didn't cast the clay aside for another piece but continued to work this lump into the vessel he envisioned. The invitation to Tass and to us is the same: Surrender and be remade.

In a radical way, Tass surrendered to the Potter, and we can trace the fruits of his life and ministry back to his transformative encounter with Jesus.

The same is true for Tita, Farai, Jo Anne, and each of the other leaders we interviewed. While their Holy Spirit encounters may not have been as dramatic as Tass's, these leaders each shared about a surrender to Jesus. They reached the end of their abilities and looked up. That is when they were given courage to continue stepping into the brokenness around them. God is the One who provided transformation in their communities and love for the people they served.

To give the impression that these are exceptional people would not only be a false rendering of their stories, but it would miss the entire message of the gospel. These leaders are not heroes of their own stories. Instead, each of them acknowledged reaching a point in their journeys where they came to the end of their own strength and reached out to God in desperation. Surrender came when they had no choice but to look up. *This* became the defining moment of their lives.

At the core, their stories—and ours—reflect a powerful Redeemer at work.

Our own efforts yield disappointments and dead ends. Yet these moments of desperation can lead to the most beautiful moments of transformation as we surrender and submit.

Tass's story is not about superficial change but supernatural transformation. He couldn't have made this radical about-face on his own; he is a remade person—just as we are each invited to become. Tass concludes, "It's God's heart that makes a difference, not us."

Application Questions

1. What areas of life do you tend to hold more tightly and struggle to surrender? Why?

2. What would it look like to believe that the Holy Spirit can work in our lives as we surrender everything to Christ?

3. Consider how Tass's surrender not only impacted him but also led to reconciliation between Jews and Arabs. How might your surrender impact others?

CHAPTER 10
COMMITMENT

Intentions must mature into commitments if we are to become persons with definition, with character, with substance. The mark of a certain kind of genius is the ability and energy to keep returning to the same task relentlessly, imaginatively, curiously, for a lifetime.

—Eugene Peterson[1]

Perhaps more than any other nation, Haiti has left an indelible mark on me (Peter).

Haiti was the first place where I led a short-term mission trip, igniting my passion for Christ-centered economic development. It is also the place where I literally believed my life was going to end.

I had spent several days visiting savings groups HOPE International initiated in Miragoane, a port town in western Haiti. These savings groups were designed to help Haitian parents launch small businesses so they could provide for their families. As we neared the end of the trip, our small team was traveling back to the capital city three hours away when we came across a line of cars stopped at a roadblock. A group of men had blocked the road with two giant buses in protest of the government's failure to deliver promised electricity to the community.

So we waited . . . and waited . . . and waited. As time passed, we realized we were going to miss our flights—and the urgent priorities awaiting us back home—if we didn't find a creative way around this obstacle.

Eager to help, Vitol, our driver and guide, stepped out of the car to see if anything could be done. Moments later he returned with a local community member, who claimed to know the protesters and promised he could navigate the blockade for us. The few dollars he required for his services seemed like a good investment.

Sitting behind the wheel and laying on the horn, our new driver carefully wove around the buses. But a hundred yards farther down the road, we faced a more difficult barrier: a truck with slashed tires blocking the way. There was also a car that had gotten stuck in the ditch in an attempt to squeeze past, which only extended the blockade.

There was no way through.

So our driver turned down a side road, hoping to bypass the barricade. After passing an eerily empty police station, we heard shouting as a group of protesters ran toward us, obviously upset by our attempted work-around. Turns out our decision to circumnavigate the roadblock was not a wise one. The mob swirled around our car. Ahead, a man pulled a pistol from his pocket and cocked it. Screaming in Creole, he rushed toward our car.

I said something courageous like "Oh dear!" while the team ducked their heads and prayed.

After a heated argument, the driver and gun-waving protester settled on a price, and we continued on our way. (A loaded gun is a powerful negotiating tool.)

Shaken but unharmed, we returned to the capital city and caught our plane just in time. Settling in my seat, I thought about my family and alternative ways to provide for them.

But as we took off, my thoughts returned to Vitol. While he said that he would wait a day for the protest to subside, I knew he would inevitably have to get back in his car, drive the same road, and pass through the same community.

And it wasn't just Vitol. HOPE International's staff in Haiti routinely face similar encounters. These men and women are talented and well-educated leaders. They could leave and find jobs elsewhere. Safe jobs with better pay. They are not serving in Haiti because they have to; they're serving in Haiti because they choose to.

Why?

It's a question I asked then and continue to ask today. Why does their resolve and hopefulness seem far more secure than my own? My desire to learn from the enduring hope of the women and men I have met during my tenure at HOPE International culminated in this book.

Based on personal experiences and a career in international development, many of my heroes are the people who refuse to run away, even though they have valid reasons and myriad opportunities to do so. People who decide to drive back when they could grab a seat beside me on the next flight out. People full of love for their brothers and sisters, who work for the betterment of their communities. People of commitment with roots that run deep.

People like Edouard Lassegue.

Launching a School

In a nation where only 10% of students finish high school, Edouard was among the fortunate few. His father's career as a civil engineer sufficiently provided for their family, making it possible for Edouard and his three siblings to attend school. "We were not rich, but neither were we poor," he shares.

Edouard's brother planned to follow in his dad's footsteps and become a civil engineer, while Edouard determined to become a doctor. Though Edouard liked the plan, a new trajectory began when in his teenage years he committed his life to the Lord at a neighborhood Bible club.

The Bible club not only opened his eyes to the life-saving message of the gospel but also gave him the opportunity to discover his leadership skills. Over the next few months, he was put in charge of organizing activities, teaching classes, and speaking to large groups.

At seventeen, Edouard was sitting under a mango tree during summer camp when he sensed the Lord speak to him a familiar verse in Luke 12:48: "When someone has been given much, much will be required in return; and when someone has been entrusted with much, even more will be required."

"It hit me like a ton of bricks," Edouard reflects. "All of a sudden, it was as if the Lord was showing me all He had given me—from being born in a family that could afford education to hearing the gospel message at a young age to taking part in all of these leadership experiences. God had given me so much."

With a deep sense of privilege, Edouard sought a way to give back to his nation. As he prayed about his next steps, he believed that education and church planting were the best ways to help shape the future of Haiti.

Edouard felt confident about this newfound direction and approached his family with his change of plans. But the idea of pastoring a church and leading a Christian school did not generate enthusiastic support from his parents. Surprised to learn that their son was choosing a far less lucrative career path, they adamantly opposed his aspirations. It wasn't just about the money, however, as they had seen church leaders abuse their positions. Edouard's cousin was especially cynical: "All pastors are crooks. Before you know it, you'll be just like one of them."

Undeterred, Edouard set off on his new career path, which temporarily led him out of Haiti. Just eighteen years old, Edouard had a dream and a one-way ticket to study in the United States. Through Bible club connections, a church in Florida had agreed to sponsor Edouard's college education to earn the degree he needed before starting a school in Haiti.

For five years, Edouard studied in Florida and South Carolina, never losing his focus on returning to his country. After graduating with a master's in school administration, he did just that, once again surprising his family. "Why didn't you just stay in the U.S.?" they questioned.

He never forgot the clarity of his mission in life. "I've been given a lot," Edouard shares. "How could I not find a way to give back to my nation?"

Dealing with Discouragement

"If you don't have patience, don't go into ministry," recommends Eris Labady, founder and board chair of Parole et Action ("Word and

Deed"), a development organization in Haiti. "Especially in this country, we need barrels of it."

Edouard agrees. "Haiti can be a tough place," he says, admitting that there have been many seasons when he has questioned his calling and become disillusioned with the Church. "When the going gets tough, you can't just look around you or you'll be discouraged. You have to look up to your heavenly Father." Throughout his career, Edouard has routinely needed to rely on his deep roots and commitment to Christ as an antidote to disappointment. On top of working with Compassion International and pastoring his church in Haiti, Edouard fulfilled his dream of starting a school. Together, he and his wife, Gina, launched the school in 1992 with a mission to provide a Christ-centered education to all children, including those who have difficulty paying school fees.

The school started in their home with fourteen students. For many years, the funds collected from fees and tuition were insufficient to pay teachers and cover their expenses. Edouard and Gina used their own resources to cover the shortfall. Even after continued social and political unrest caused many of their relatives and friends to flee the country, they remained committed to the school and to their country.

"People usually associate Haiti with charity, as if nothing can happen without outside funding," Edouard explains. They were determined to prove otherwise. To sustain their vision, the Lassegues wanted to make sure the school was self-supporting. They were convinced if they offered a good product, parents would be willing to make the necessary sacrifices for their children.

Balancing self-sufficiency with a welcoming posture toward all students is a delicate line to walk, particularly in a country like Haiti with rampant poverty. When tuition was adjusted for inflation, parents were not always understanding. This tension reached a new height when parents of the students took legal action and sued Edouard and Gina for raising the cost of tuition.

The Lassegues had started this school as a grateful response to God's blessings—and had sacrificed much to support it. Many of the families had sent multiple children to the school and had known Edouard for over a decade. This legal action against them felt like a very personal attack on their family, a deep betrayal from the people they had spent their lives serving.

Edouard had found a way to handle challenges from the government, natural disasters, and corruption, but this attack from the community hit particularly hard.

"When we heard the news, my wife and I sat in our home and cried. We asked God if this school was really worth it. If this was really what He was calling us to."

As they prayed, God led them back to their initial call and commitment. "The whole experience caused us to ask ourselves, 'What are we here for? Are we here to make a name for ourselves, or are we here to make an impact on the next generation?'"

They wiped their tears and rolled up their sleeves. Despite the disappointment and discouragement, they remained committed to providing an excellent education for students.

When we asked Edouard how he kept going in the midst of this and myriad other obstacles, he shared a story he had been told of a girl carrying her younger brother on her back. The boy was unable to walk, so the girl would carry him wherever she went, at times hardly able to walk herself. When others looked at the situation, they'd say, "Oh, this is terrible. That's such a heavy burden for you to carry."

She responded simply, "But he's my brother."[2]

"The sense of duty is heavy," Edouard acknowledges. "There are days I've asked God to relieve me of my duty, relieve me of my love—for sometimes it's just too painful." Ultimately, it's commitment rooted in love that pushes him to this level of sacrifice.

Over time, the school grew to over five hundred students, from kindergarten through high school. Every year the school must refuse dozens of applications because the demand for their work exceeds their current capacity. Today, many graduates become pastors, entrepreneurs, artists, and doctors, serving the Lord in their families, churches, and communities. These alumni are often guest speakers in chapel and school gatherings, inspiring current students to keep their eyes on the Lord, to study well, and to embrace their own callings. One particular affirmation for the Lassegues came when their own daughter felt the Lord's call to continue the work of the school; she returned to Haiti with a graduate degree after completing her studies in the U.S. She is now leading the ministry and overseeing its expansion.

While Edouard sees the difficulties, he views them through the lens of love, hope, and trust. "If I can trust the gospel to save my soul, I trust that it can also transform the country of Haiti."

Beautiful Obligation

Like Edouard, Jeremiah's story begins with a clear calling from the Lord: "I knew you before I formed you in your mother's womb. Before you were born I set you apart and appointed you as my prophet to the nations."[3]

From the beginning of time, God knew Jeremiah intimately and called him to be a prophet. But, like many of us, Jeremiah felt utterly inadequate and ill-prepared for the mission God had called him to. *Surely God must have made a mistake!* In the very next verse, Jeremiah responds, "O Sovereign LORD . . . I can't speak for you! I'm too young!"[4]

Scholars estimate that Jeremiah was a teenager when God called him, a similar age as Edouard when he sensed God speaking to him under the mango tree. Taking an honest look at himself, Jeremiah saw his youth, his inexperience, his lack of social standing,[5] and his inadequacies. He wasn't old enough. Capable enough. Brave enough. Strong enough. Wise enough. Eloquent enough. "If we look at ourselves and are absolutely honest, we are always inadequate," writes Eugene Peterson. "Of course, we are not always honest."[6] But a posture of honest humility—in Jeremiah and in us—invites God to display His power.

God clarifies that the mission would not rest on Jeremiah's strengths nor his abilities. He called Jeremiah to reject the idol of self-sufficiency and look upward: "Don't say, 'I'm too young,' for you must go wherever I send you and say whatever I tell you. And don't be afraid of the people, for I will be with you and will protect you. I, the LORD, have spoken!"[7]

Acutely aware of his own weaknesses, Jeremiah had no choice but to rely on God's strength.

Edouard and the other global leaders we learned from have a deep understanding of their inadequacies and weaknesses that initially feels incongruous with their even deeper resolve and commitment to their mission. Yet their humility allows them to focus on God's strength and embrace His promise: "My power works best in weakness."[8] That same humility enables them to root their commitment not in their own gritty resolve but in *God's* commitment.

It isn't just that Edouard has a heart for Haiti; Edouard knows that God has a heart for Haiti. As he works to address challenging circumstances in Haiti, he isn't working alone but rather accepting an invitation to join God in His ongoing work of renewal. Edouard holds a beautiful obligation and commitment to his nation because he trusts that both he and Haiti are held by God.

In 2004, when Edouard received an unexpected opportunity to take on the challenge of overseeing all of Compassion International's operations in Central America and the Caribbean, he initially refused the offer. The position would require his relocation to the United States, and it felt like a departure from his calling and commitment to Haiti.

> The leaders we interviewed believe that they are called to God first and then invited to commit to a specific cause or community: reflecting His heart for justice, poverty alleviation, reconciliation, and other forms of restoration.

But as he prayed about the job offer and discussed it with senior leaders at Compassion, Edouard began to see that this opportunity was not in conflict with his calling but rather an extension of it. God would use him to serve and bless the people of Haiti—and many other nations as well.

The leaders we interviewed believe, as Edouard came to see, that they are called to God first and then invited to commit to a specific cause or community: reflecting His heart for justice, poverty alleviation, reconciliation, and other forms of restoration. Edouard followed God's leading and faithfully stewarded the opportunities God provided.

In difficult moments of drought, commitments keep us turning upward, pursuing goals that are absolutely impossible in our own strength or capacity. And that's precisely the point; we are not acting in our strength alone.

In our conversations with Edouard, it became abundantly clear that he was doing something he knew would be impossible in his own strength. Leaders who set out to address the challenging issues in our world will always be inadequate, eventually overwhelmed by the enormity of the problems and the complexity of the solutions. Yet it's precisely this awareness of our limitations that drives us to the end of our humanistic self-help projects. It causes us to call out to the only One who can truly save.

Leaders who live with enduring hope—leaders like Edouard—are marked by deep roots that reach Living Water. In seasons of joy and struggle, Edouard returns to the moment he experienced God's grace in a Bible club and the commitment he made under a mango tree. These moments offered clarity on his life's work to impact future generations in Haiti and beyond, and they continue to offer clarity and perspective on his God-given mission today.

Application Questions

1. Why do you think it is so challenging for people to commit in today's world?
2. Edouard mentioned that his deep love for Haiti and his duty to serve its people are intertwined. Has God placed a deep love for a specific cause, location, or people in your heart?

3. What is holding you back from committing to that cause?

4. What would it look like in your life to follow our "beautiful obligation" to serve others?

5. How can we remind ourselves of the importance of our commitment in the midst of challenges?

CHAPTER 11
OUTWARD

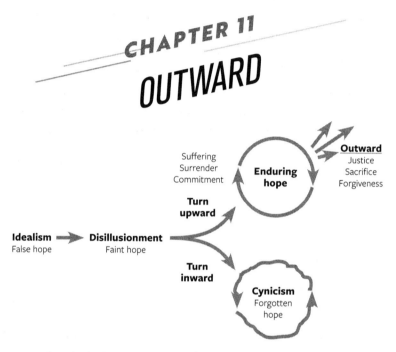

Soon after the holiness of God was lost, then the claims of neighborly love were also lost.

—Walter Brueggemann[1]

I n Egypt and then in the wilderness, God's people experienced 443 years of waiting and hoping for a vision that finally would be realized in the Promised Land. When the Israelites arrived at their long-awaited destination, they had an opportunity to return to their original purpose and mission. God promised Abraham, the patriarch of this nation, "I will bless you and make your name great, *so that you will be a blessing. . . .* In you all the families of the earth shall be blessed."[2]

108

From day one in the Promised Land, God established the expectation that the Israelites would not only care for their own but also extend their newfound stability and security to all who would enter their territory. His laws for the people of Israel included provisions for foreigners and strangers among them.[3]

Joshua Jipp, a theologian and professor at Trinity Evangelical Divinity School, describes the uniqueness of the Promised Land this way: "The importance of Israel's laws protecting the immigrant mark God's people out as distinctive, since no comparable particular concern for the immigrant is found in the law-codes of Israel's neighbors."[4]

The Israelites were to create the inverse of Egypt, establishing the Promised Land as a place of refuge and provision—not slavery and oppression—for the vulnerable. For this reason, again and again, God

> The Israelites were to create the inverse of Egypt, establishing the Promised Land as a place of refuge and provision—not slavery and oppression—for the vulnerable.

reminds them they were once slaves in Egypt.[5] "True justice must be given to foreigners living among you and to orphans. . . . Always remember that you were slaves in Egypt and that the LORD your God redeemed you from your slavery. That is why I have given you this command."[6]

Instead of relentlessly pursuing wealth and power, the Israelites had laws to protect the most vulnerable. Instead of using humans as dispensable objects, they were to treat others with dignity and worth. They were not to mirror the injustice they had experienced in Egypt but to model a countercultural commitment to justice. They were freed from abuse and freed to reflect God's love. Although they pursued it inconsistently and imperfectly, this mission to establish a kingdom of God's design was the Israelites' road map.[7]

But how quickly we veer off course. How often we use power and privilege to serve ourselves and not others, the oppressed becoming the oppressors.[8]

The nations of Israel and Judah lost their way in the Promised Land. They settled down, became comfortable, and followed in the pattern of their Egyptian oppressors. They lost sight of their mission to be a people of blessing by caring for the vulnerable.

God always sees and cares when there is injustice, so He anointed Jeremiah to rebuke Judah (as well as other nations and kingdoms)[9] for turning their backs on God and their mission. There was blood on their hands and stubborn pride in their hearts.[10]

In Jeremiah, God rebukes the powerful—including the nation's kings—for shirking their responsibility to love justice and mercy.

> "This is what the LORD says: Be fair-minded and just. Do what is right!
> Help those who have been robbed; rescue them from their oppressors.
> Quit your evil deeds! Do not mistreat foreigners, orphans, and widows.
> Stop murdering the innocent!"[11]

God speaks through Jeremiah to rebuke King Jehoiakim, whom he contrasts unflatteringly with the example of his father, King Josiah. Despite ascending to the throne at the age of eight, King Josiah "was just and right in all his dealings."[12]

King Jehoiakim pursued a different legacy. He focused inward, obsessing on what he could gain and not on what he could give. He mirrored the pattern of the pharaoh, not of the gracious and compassionate God his father served. The Lord reminds Jehoiakim that Josiah "gave justice and help to the poor and needy," challenging, "Isn't that what it means to know me?"[13] The rebuke continues, "But you! You have eyes only for greed and dishonesty! You murder the innocent, oppress the poor, and reign ruthlessly."[14]

Under King Jehoiakim, the nation abandoned its mission to repair brokenness and extend God's shalom. They no longer resembled a nation set apart through worship of God and service of neighbor. They had stopped looking up to God and out to their neighbors, instead closing their ears and their eyes to the needs of others.

Later in the book of Jeremiah, when some of God's people find themselves exiled in Babylon, Jeremiah encourages them to retain the mission although they have lost the land. He exhorts them to settle into their new homes and seek the welfare of the city.[15]

We cannot miss the radical, countercultural nature of this suggestion for these exiles. He asked them to seek the welfare of the very city where they were persecuted. To follow Jeremiah's encouragement was to admit that their hope was not in an imminent return to Jerusalem: They could rediscover their mission far away from the Promised Land. Jeremiah encouraged them to embrace an enduring hope rooted in God's unfailing character, which was not contingent on place. Their hope belonged not in an unshakable city but in an unshakable God.

Rather than looking inward at their *weakness* and giving up or looking inward at their *strength* and trying to overcome, Jeremiah encouraged the exiles to look upward to the only One who could provide hope—then turn outward to share His love and blessings, even with their oppressors.

This mission has not changed. Loving others is not peripheral; it has always been central to our mission and inextricably linked to our love of God. It is a call independent of the place we inhabit or even how we are treated. It extends not just to "our people" but to all people. Jesus' words that challenged Tass challenge each one of us: "You have heard the law that says, 'Love your neighbor' and hate your enemy. But I say, love your enemies! Pray for those who persecute you! In that way, you will be acting as true children of your Father in heaven."[16]

The mission hasn't changed—but neither has the inward pull. We feel ourselves gravitate away from courageous, outward-leading compassion. We subtly succumb to the inward pull when we decide our organizations should prioritize their institutional well-being over the people served. We stop risking, wanting to play it safe. We more overtly succumb when we pursue power, platform, and privilege instead of sacrifice and service. But children of God have always been called to focus outward: to seek the welfare of the places we inhabit and the people we encounter. To serve rooted in our experience and understanding of God's grace rather than our own strength.

Focusing outward without looking upward inevitably leads to cynicism, burnout, and stagnation. Our service cannot sustain our hope; our hope in Christ sustains our service.

Even in exile, we are to be people of faith, hope, and love. There's a reason these three are often linked in Scripture. In Paul's first letter to the church at Thessalonica, he explores their impact on our service, writing, "We remember before our God and Father your work produced

> ## Our service cannot sustain our hope; our hope in Christ sustains our service.

by faith, your labor prompted by love, and your endurance inspired by hope in our Lord Jesus Christ."[17] Faith, hope, and love are inextricably interwoven.

Rooted faith nourishes enduring hope. Love prompts—and hope sustains—our labor. Love inspires leaders to ask, "How many kids are in foster care?" And then, "What can we do about it?" It prompts them to ask, "How many families are in poverty?" and then step out in courage to decrease that number. Loving God and loving our neighbors cannot be separated; these commands comprise the mission of God's people.

The following three stories highlight leaders who turned upward, leading to outward expressions of love toward overlooked, underserved, and vulnerable populations. Rooted in Christ, they are leaders who follow God's leading. Who work for justice. Who sacrifice for others. Who forgive. Who serve. Who love beyond reason or reciprocity.

These leaders love the King and work faithfully to see the Kingdom come. They turn upward, then outward, leading to justice in Oklahoma (chapter 12), sacrifice in India (chapter 13), and forgiveness in Lebanon (chapter 14).

Application Questions

1. What does it mean to be a people set apart "to bless the nations of the world"?
2. Like Israel having once been slaves in Egypt, how can we remember that God has redeemed us?
3. How does knowing the redemption of Christ for our lives change the way we live?
4. Is your tendency to live inwardly or outwardly? Why?
5. What would it look like to "seek the welfare of the city" where God has placed you?

CHAPTER 12

JUSTICE

Erase the effects of red-lining, systemic racism, and the ravages of generational poverty and we will see a great leveling of the playing field for all kids.

—Chris Brewster, Superintendent, Santa Fe South Charter School, Oklahoma City, OK[1]

In 1848, Horace Mann, a pioneer of American public schools, famously called education "the great equalizer."[2] Mann himself was not well taught as a child, but his independent studies, combined with the tutelage of a local minister, helped him gain admission to Brown University and go on to law school, later becoming secretary of the Massachusetts State Board of Education and a representative in the U.S. Congress. Education was Mann's great passion, and he viewed the subject with tremendous optimism.

In 2011, Arne Duncan, U.S. Secretary of Education under President Barack Obama, paraphrased Mann's hope-filled assertion, declaring, "In America, education is still the great equalizer."[3] It's a noble aspiration, but parents, teachers, administrators, and education reformers alike often decry the inequities riddling the very system entrusted to equalize.

A 2012 article in *The Atlantic* summarized the problem well: "If the great equalizer's ability to equalize America is dwindling, it's not because education is growing less important in the modern economy. Paradoxically, it's precisely because schooling is now even more important."[4] In the United States, school funding comes from three levels: state (averaging 47%), local (averaging 45%), and federal (averaging just 8%).[5] This system of highly localized funding creates islands of opportunity amid oceans of inequality.

Though the 1954 Supreme Court decision in *Brown v. Board of Education* banned segregation of public schools by race more than half a century ago, American schools remain largely segregated—by income and, de facto, by race. A recent report found that more than half of U.S. students attend racially concentrated districts. These districts comprise either over 75% white or over 75% nonwhite students. And separate still isn't equal. In 2016, districts predominantly serving students of color received $23 billion less in funding than mostly white districts, despite serving the same number of students. The impact can be easier to comprehend on a smaller scale: Nonwhite districts averaged $2,200 less per student than predominantly white districts.[6]

In some places, the disparities are even starker. Just outside the city of Philadelphia—the poorest big city in the nation[7]—the Lower Merion school district increased education funding 87% between 2000 and 2015. They now spend more than $23,000 per student. Philadelphia, just a handful of miles away, spends less than half as much to reach their less advantaged student population.[8]

Parents with means self-select into high-spending, high-performing districts. As families flock to strong schools, home values soar, pricing out lower-income residents. In the process, resources are further concentrated in already well-funded districts, while poorer districts grow poorer still. Bluntly put, "It's an academic arms race."[9]

It's a familiar dynamic to Chris Brewster, superintendent of schools at Santa Fe South—the largest brick-and-mortar charter school in Oklahoma—and a vocal advocate for school choice. "Families with money have always had a choice," Chris says. "And families without money, of all colors, don't have a choice."[10]

Chris didn't set out to become an apologist for education reform, but we all want what's best for the people we love, and his God-given love of children and commitment to following the Holy Spirit's leading left him no other option.

Salty Leadership

The afternoon we spoke, Chris sat in a quiet office, the closed door barely keeping at bay the bustle on the other side. Every so often the phone would ring, an indication of the many demands on his time and attention.

Behind his desk sits a shelf that's crowded but not cluttered—filled with books, binders, and objects serving as reminders of what matters. He displays pictures of his family—his wife, Christi, and their eight children, four biological and four adopted. There's a vibrant sunrise on canvas, composed of tiny thumbprints: a gift from Santa Fe South's youngest learners. It neighbors a less cheerful, though perhaps even more motivating, reminder: a piece of art created by a young man once homeless in Nebraska. Chris describes him as a "brilliant man" who struggles with mental illness. "The system failed him," he reflects.

On the edge of the shelf, a sign with boldface letters proclaims BE SALTY. It was a gift from a teenager who told Chris he was salty—in a good way. The idea resonated with Chris. As a bi-vocational minister and school administrator, he preached his first-ever sermon on being the salt of the earth. In Scripture, Chris sees salt as a healer and preserver. And that's a role he embraces wholeheartedly.

Chris never envisioned himself as the superintendent of a charter school district serving 3,600 students with a waiting list half as long. Raised in the Philippines, he is the child of missionaries and describes his parents' "lives of service." They believed—and taught—that Christians were to use the talents and opportunities they had been given to extend and expand God's Kingdom. Chris grew up thinking this mindset was common to all Christians. As he contemplated his own career path, Chris looked to the people who had most impacted him. Apart from his parents, those were his teachers and coaches, so he returned

116

to the United States—to Oklahoma Baptist University, the very place his parents first met—and studied teaching.

Prior to returning for college, Chris had spent limited time in the U.S., visiting only briefly when his family was on furlough. Though Chris had little firsthand exposure to American culture, his parents had taught "American ideals" like freedom, bravery, and opportunity, so he came with great expectations. He found the reality, however, to be "less Norman Rockwell."[11]

"I saw bigotry, and I saw materialism and a class system that I wasn't really prepared to handle," Chris remembers. It was a shock to his system to realize "what it meant to be an American in America."[12] The reality never sat comfortably with Chris, who, in the words of his friend and fellow Oklahoma City pastor John-Mark Hart, "is driven by a sincere love for people, a passion for justice, and a deep faith in Jesus."

Graduating as a newly minted teacher, Chris saw an opportunity to confront some of these evils by educating and mentoring students in a gang-ridden, written-off, inner-city school. He took a job at Capitol Hill High School in a "radically underserved" Oklahoma City community. There, he coached wrestling, soccer, and volleyball and directed a choir notable for its size—270 members—if not skill. Chris loved the kids, but about six years into his teaching career, he reached a watershed moment. "I decided there just wasn't any real hope in the system," he says, describing a "gristmill" that "took kids in and churned them out" with little semblance of an education.

This is as good a time as any to mention Chris's ambivalence toward adults. "My favorite human beings are teenagers," he says. "Adults I divide into two groups: those who are good for kids and everybody else." He chafed against the idea of being part of a system where students weren't nurtured and weren't flourishing. "This cannot be what I'm supposed to spend my one precious life on," Chris remembers thinking.

This Cannot Be . . .

His first instinct wasn't to fight the system but to flee it. Chris began investigating other options: perhaps international missions or serving in a church. But then he spoke with Dr. Raul Font, his principal and mentor—and a fellow educator who loved his students. Font encouraged Chris to pursue an administrative degree. The idea of further embedding himself in a broken system didn't entice Chris. But when he "reluctantly obeyed," he began to see bright spots in education across the country—places where real academic, social, and emotional gains were being made with similar student populations. "I began to see glimmers of hope," he says. "When I got that degree, I was reminded that our God is a God of hope, and He desires for our communities to thrive. He desires for our children to thrive. He desires for our cities to be restored." This was no time to quit.

Chris's first administrative post was one zip code and a world away from Capitol Hill High School. From 98% of students qualifying for free or reduced lunch at Capitol Hill to 2% at Deer Creek High School, Chris saw the sharp disparities between attending school in the city and the suburbs. One—largely Hispanic—population lacked opportunity. Twenty minutes away, diversity was lacking but opportunity abounded. According to the Educational Opportunity Project, an initiative aimed at harnessing data to improve educational opportunity, students in Oklahoma City schools test at 1.62 grade levels *below* the U.S. average. Students at Deer Creek, by contrast, score 1.37 grade levels *above* the U.S. average—a differential of nearly three grade levels.[13]

"I began to understand the embedded racism and bias in the system. I didn't understand how to unravel this thing. I just knew that the disparity was stark and that this was not pleasing to our God." Of that, Chris could be confident.

Throughout Scripture, God concerns himself with justice. The Israelites were to be a people set apart, not to oppress the nations of the world—as was common practice among dominant nations of the day—but to bless them.[14] They were to be marked by their concern for the poor and weak among them. The Torah, God's law for ancient Israel, instituted checks against oppression.[15] "For the LORD your God . . . shows no partiality and cannot be bribed. He ensures that the orphans and widows receive justice. He shows love to the foreigners living among you and gives them food and clothing. So you, too, must show love to foreigners, for you yourselves were once foreigners in the land of Egypt," God instructed Moses.[16] Several hundred years later, the expectation hadn't changed for the people of Judah.

While the central theme in Jeremiah is a call for God's people to return to Him, a closely related theme interspersed throughout the book is a call for justice. Much of the text promises judgment, but in Jeremiah 7, God plainly offers the people an alternative: "But I will be merciful only if you stop your evil thoughts and deeds and start treating each other with justice; only if you stop exploiting foreigners, orphans, and widows; only if you stop your murdering; and only if you stop harming yourselves by worshiping idols. Then I will let you stay in this land that I gave to your ancestors to keep forever."[17]

As God's words strongly imply, following other gods was to the Israelites' harm—not only in severing their relationship with Him but also in distorting their relationships with one another.

Different gods were seen to have different priorities, and only Yahweh expressed particular concern for the vulnerable. "Ba'al supports survival and security and subordinates concern for those on the social margins. Yahweh's priorities are just the opposite: justice for those without power or status takes precedence over survival and security," writes John M. Bracke, professor of biblical studies at Eden Theological Seminary.[18]

In Jeremiah 9:24, God outlines His priorities. "I am the LORD, who exercises kindness, justice and righteousness on earth, for in these I delight" (NIV). Throughout the book of Jeremiah, "Failure to enact justice either by actively exploiting others for personal gain or by failing to care for those who are marginalized signals a broken relationship with God," says Samuel Hildebrandt.[19]

Jeremiah's words concerning justice apply to all the people of Judah, but the book also contains many directives specific to Judah's kings: those in positions of power and influence.[20] Jeremiah offers positive admonitions to "do what is just and right" as well as prohibitions against mistreating "foreigners, orphans, and widows."[21] The implication is that those of us in positions of relative privilege must steward our influence for the good of the vulnerable. Where justice is concerned, there are not only sins of commission but also sins of omission. To emulate God's heart for justice we must not only avoid actively exploiting or oppressing others but also refuse to passively benefit from an unjust status quo.

"Justice" can feel like such a large and overwhelming pursuit. There's wisdom in the Jewish teaching, "You are not required to complete the task, but neither are you free to desist from it."[22]

Pastor Hart identifies Chris's deep trust and faith in God as the source of his courage to "take risks and make sacrifices." Hart reflects, "He would rather be uncomfortable while caring for hurting people than be comfortable while indifferent to the needs of others."

As we seek justice, we can begin by asking God to make us uncomfortable with our comfort. What injustices do we readily overlook? Which lives have we been willing to treat with less value than our own? How are we benefiting from unjust systems? How can we look outward?

We can also pray for and seek opportunities to broaden the circle of those we love to include others from backgrounds very unlike our own: whether that's refugees, those with disabilities, individuals of different races or socioeconomic status, or those most vulnerable to the effects of climate change. When those we love are suffering harm, we cannot

> When we love those harmed by unjust systems or trampled in pursuit of others' gain, we become natural and passionate advocates for justice.

stand by silently. When we love those harmed by unjust systems or trampled in pursuit of others' gain, we become natural and passionate advocates for justice.

The status quo wasn't likely to harm Chris Brewster—a light-skinned, college-educated man with a stable income and good health. But he knew it was harming people beloved by God. "It was so disconcerting that our society would say this is okay," he reflects. Rather than turning a blind eye, he put his shoulder to the plow and got to work.

"Regardless of whether this situation is my fault, it's my responsibility to work toward correcting it," he says.

Unloved

Chris believes that, as a society, we fundamentally don't love children. The accusation riles listeners, putting them on the defensive. Chris clarifies: He thinks we love *our own* children well. Perhaps we even love the children in close proximity to our own. But there are other children in our orbits for whom we've abdicated responsibility—and it is these children Chris posits are not loved well and are, in fact, not well. They are failing.

He references the Swahili greeting exchanged between Maasai warriors, *Kasserian Ingera*, meaning, "And how are the children?"[23] "The response is, if the children are well, it speaks to the entirety of society. If the children are not well, it also speaks to the entirety of society. Until we can say in Oklahoma City, for example, that all our children are well, we haven't done well enough."

In February 2001, Chris got one of those phone calls that changes the course of your life. "Would you consider launching a charter school for under-resourced students?" the caller queried. Chris was just demoralized—yet optimistic—enough to say yes.

He had never opened a school before. He didn't exactly know how, but he had seen failing schools. He had seen "horrific places to be a child," and, not even knowing what he didn't know, he told himself, "Surely we can do better" for Oklahoma City's children.

Santa Fe South opened the following August in a rented church facility. Oklahoma's charter schools are eligible for state funding, but they do not receive local property tax funding, so Chris would, in effect, be serving a more challenging student population with significantly less funding.[24] Santa Fe South would get about 76 cents for every dollar of funding that typical public schools receive.[25] The trade-off? More freedom to work outside the established education system, customizing their approach to fit the student population. They wouldn't be dealing with teachers' unions or tenures. Their staff would work on one-year renewable contracts, continuously earning the right to keep their jobs.

They'd extend the school day, implement more rigorous graduation requirements, establish a strict attendance policy, and value families as the first teachers. Most of all, they would love their students.

Santa Fe South had no books, computers, athletic space, equipment, or track record. "We didn't have anything that should have drawn anybody to our school," Chris says. And yet, when the school opened, they were not only fully enrolled with 120 students, but they also had a waiting list.

Chris thought they had successfully communicated to their neighborhood constituency just how amazing the school would be—and realized only later that the parents may have had much lower expectations than that.

Perhaps not even daring to expect, the parents hoped Santa Fe South would be an improvement over their home districts, which were "basically burning down." The gravity of the situation settled on Chris: "It was a crushing realization that our community was in such a crisis that they would risk their children at a school like ours. We had nothing. But we were still a better bet with their most precious possession."

Superpowers

As Santa Fe South continued to grow, the school needed a space of its own. Chris approached a bank to ask for a loan. It took some convincing, but when Chris thought the loan officer had finally been persuaded, the banker's next words stopped Chris in his tracks: "We're going to take out a life insurance policy on you." Chris thought it was a joke, but the banker was all business. They made loans of this sort based not on the institution but the leader, he explained. Putting it bluntly, "If you get hit by a truck, we need to have a backstop."

Chris describes it as a moment of crisis. He realized that, as a leader, he had left his school without a life insurance policy. "I called it my work ethic, but my desire to do everything and be in charge of everything and to be in control of everything was actually the most significant point of weakness in my organization. I was creating a school that was deeply flawed because it was relying on my abilities." Chris recognized it as hubris, and he committed to changing it.

He sees a continuum in which idealism pairs with ignorance and describes a "nasty irony" where the more you gain in wisdom and knowledge, the more you lose in confidence. "Every time you mess up in a way that causes stress or harm to your organization, it chips away at your confidence. It's a balance between maintaining humility and feeling defeated."

In these moments of defeat, Chris's wife of nearly thirty years has been especially influential. When he questions his calling or qualifications for addressing the omnipresent challenges facing a school like Santa Fe South, she never attempts to assuage his concerns. Rather, she suggests they pray together: "We have to make sure you are the right person for this, that this is where God has you," she tells him. "Her quiet confidence that the Spirit will lead has always been something very consoling to me," Chris says.

With prayerful consideration, Chris has built a team of people who excel in areas where he is weak, loosening his grip on the growing organization he manages. Letting go has empowered Chris to uncover his true "superpower": hiring exceptional people. He's now fully confident that Santa Fe South can thrive in his absence. "This institution isn't going to stand or fall on my strength or frailties." The team of leaders and teachers surrounding him has contributed to building a school that is safe, culturally relevant, and relentless in its love for their students.

And their impact is extending beyond the school and into the broader community. Pastor Hart shares, "Thousands of people in south Oklahoma City deeply respect Chris Brewster because they know that he genuinely cares about them, their children, and their community. He has worked tirelessly for many years to help people in south Oklahoma City reach their full, God-given potential. Now many of the students he has served are adults, parents, leaders, and community servants. The long-term impact of his deep investment in generations of children is immeasurable."

Taking Sides

Salt can heal and preserve—but it can also corrode. Chris gives the impression of someone who is simultaneously winsome, engaging, and not afraid to take a side.

His love for children and teens has led him to take some unpopular stances. When the group Pastors for Oklahoma Kids took a stance against school choice, Chris—who is also a pastor—fired back that denying choice benefits the status quo, while granting choice benefits the vulnerable.[26] When bars and casinos opened while schools remained shuttered to many students during the coronavirus pandemic, Chris called out everyone from business owners to the governor of Oklahoma, questioning the priorities driving those decisions.

Low Marks and High Praise

Santa Fe South is not a tremendous success by *every* measure. The state of Oklahoma gives it a report card few would flaunt: C's, D's, and F's on measures from absenteeism to English language proficiency progress and academic achievement.[28] Chris pushes back against the standards of measurement. "Unless we're trying to affirm that it was a great idea for white people to move to suburbia, affirming white flight and affirming selective admission process—unless the letter grade is only affirming that practice—then nobody is doing anything about what it's revealing," says Chris.[29]

The Educational Opportunity Project is more nuanced in its assessment. Their reporting indicates students at Santa Fe South Middle School score 1.51 grade levels below the U.S. average. But, taking into account the unequal start children are given in life, it also shows students at the school learn 16% *more* each grade than the U.S. average,[30] calling this "learning rate" score "a better indicator of school quality than average test scores, which are influenced by a range of experiences outside of school."[31]

Oklahoma's system of assessing schools forces Chris to constantly contemplate his priorities. Does he want his school to look like a success, or does he want his students to be well? "We don't filter kids out. We're one of the few charter schools that doesn't ask our kids to form around a theme or a course of study. What we contemplate, then, is not how do we bring a child in and require that they conform to a particular type of student. We contemplate what would it be like as a school community to form around the child so they're successful."

Chris works hard to avoid the common, accepted practice in academia of "culling the inputs." From selective admission of preschoolers to pushing AP and honors tracks for high schoolers, to minimum SAT scores for college admissions, these practices are focused, Chris says, not on what is best for the student but what is best for the institution. At Santa Fe South, students come as they are.

Santa Fe South operates in an area Oklahoma City's police force has dubbed "the block." Most of the city's violent crime happens here. The school draws its student population from the two most poverty-affected and highest-crime zip codes in the city. Chris has had to confront drug dealers lurking near his campus.[32] Yet he speaks of his students and their neighborhood as though the privilege of working together is all his. "It's an exciting community to be a part of. There's tremendous potential, great hope, and hard work."[33]

Walk the halls of Santa Fe South and you'll see college admissions letters plastering the walls. College is by no means a foregone conclusion for these students—many of whom will be the first in their families to attend—but it is an expectation at Santa Fe South. The expectation is backed up by support. Every student is assigned a staff member who monitors their progress. They remind students of graduation requirements, college entrance exams, and application deadlines.

And although Chris oversees the district, he continues to invest deeply in individuals. Christian Arenivar, a college freshman with a full-ride scholarship to Oklahoma Baptist—Chris's alma mater—speaks of the difference Chris made in his life as a leader and coach. He remembers Chris sacrificing time over breaks to drive him to out-of-state cross country meets. He marvels that Chris still attends his college races, cheering him on even now. "I probably would have gone the wrong route if it were not for his coaching and leadership at Santa Fe South," he reflects. "He made me see something I did not know I had in me. . . . He lit a light for me, and I just followed it and am continuing to do so."

Chris and his tremendous teachers and leaders have created a highly sought-after environment. They've had parents lie about their children's admission status and even forge birth certificates to get priority sibling status in the school's admissions lottery. "We have identified and are meeting a need that is a heart cry of our community right now," Chris says.

At Santa Fe South, the children are well. But with 1,700 children's names on an ever-growing waitlist, this is no time to quit. This is a time for an unflagging outward focus.

Application Questions

1. What do you see in your community or circles of influence that is "not pleasing to our God"?

2. Do you feel you are marked by your concern for the poor and weak? Why or why not?

3. What populations or causes can you pray for on a regular basis? What would it look like to actively seek justice for those individuals?

CHAPTER 13
SACRIFICE

Pure and genuine religion in the sight of God the Father means caring for orphans and widows in their distress and refusing to let the world corrupt you.

—James 1:27

Amara[1] knows what it is like to live with vulnerability. When James, the half brother of Jesus, talks about orphans and widows, he's talking about her. Born to a Hindu family in southern India, Amara lost both her parents before she turned two years old. Even today, she knows no details of their deaths.

The responsibility of caring for Amara and her two sisters fell to her uncle, their next of kin. Unsure if he would have the capacity to pay for their food, let alone their dowries, he saw his nieces as a liability. He took the girls on a two-day journey to the nearest orphanage and dropped them off, never to see them again.

Though abandoned by their family, Amara and her sisters were welcomed into the orphanage by a Christian woman who believed God had called her to love and care for orphaned children. In this context, Amara came to faith in Jesus. And this newfound faith became the bedrock for her life and work.

Many years later, Amara met her husband, Rahul, a church planter and evangelist, through an arranged marriage. As Christian minorities in a Hindu-majority context, Amara and Rahul stood out, but they stood together. They believed God had brought them together and imagined what He might do through their marriage and service in India.

In their early years of marriage, the couple had two sons, Riaan and Chandran. The family started planting churches and saw God at work, particularly among vulnerable communities facing extreme poverty.

At age thirty-six, Rahul prepared to travel overseas for a pastors' conference. Rahul headed to the hospital for routine pre-travel vaccinations with young Riaan by his side. But almost immediately, Rahul reacted negatively to the vaccine. He passed away within the week, leaving behind a grieving widow and two young children. At the time, Riaan was four and a half years old, and Chandran was three.

Amara, who had grown up as an orphan, was now a young widow as well.

At that time in India, Amara's story was not just unfortunate—it was devastating. Without a safety net, a widow with young children is extremely vulnerable. Disaster didn't tarry; on Wednesday the family attended Rahul's funeral, and on Friday they had to vacate their home because they couldn't pay the rent.

Yet, once again, followers of Jesus lived out "pure religion." This time, it wasn't caring for orphans, but caring for a widow and her two children.

A missionary acquaintance provided a room for the family, and though it required moving to a different town hundreds of miles away, it protected them from having to move to the slums. The invitation was lifesaving for Amara, Riaan, and Chandran.

Even though the family had avoided immediate disaster, life was difficult. Riaan remembers, "We didn't have any money. My mom didn't have a job, and we didn't have a school to attend."

Yet he saw his mother's faith—the way she confidently held on to Jesus despite bleak circumstances. "I remember her telling us, 'The Word of God is true, and it says the Lord takes care of orphans and widows. I started as an orphan; now I'm a widow.'"

Riaan continues, "She had this attitude that, somehow, God was going to make a way."

His mother's deep roots in Christ sustained the family. A year later, Amara learned of a private boarding school looking for staff. By the grace of God, she received the job—and with it a place to live and an opportunity for her sons to attend one of the best schools in the country. "God literally lifted our family up out of the ashes and put us on solid ground," Riaan reflects.

Amara's salary was only three dollars per month. But somehow it was enough.

Even with her meager income, Amara modeled extravagant generosity. After receiving her monthly salary, she would immediately set aside a portion as her tithe. And every March—the month she celebrated her anniversary at the school—she did even more. When she received that month's salary, she wouldn't even open the envelope it had arrived in. Instead, she would take it to church and drop the whole envelope in the offering plate.

Her courageous faith and sacrifice inspired her sons.

Faith vs. Fatalism

It wasn't until his teenage years that Riaan began to understand the difference between his mother's faith and the fatalism of the caste system in India.

One of his closest friends lived next door, and they would regularly play cricket and soccer together. His friend's parents cleaned the neighborhood sewers. Initially, Riaan didn't think much about their occupation. It was a job, and he knew from firsthand experience that parents did anything possible to provide for their families.

Yet Riaan began to notice a pattern. As he met other members of his friend's family, he learned that every one of them cleaned sewers. "Why do all your relatives clean the sewers?" Riaan candidly asked his friend.

The question caught his friend off guard. "That's what we're called to do," he replied simply.

"Who says?" Riaan prodded.

That day was the first time Riaan remembers hearing the word *dalit*. The lowest level of the caste system, dalit literally means "sewer cleaners" or "untouchables."

Riaan started to recognize the stark contrast between his faith in a God who created all individuals with gifts, potential, worth, and love—and a religion that doomed some to squalor from birth. It was because of his faith in Christ that Riaan—and his mother before him—was never without hope.

Escape

A few years later, Riaan and his brother graduated from high school, their tuition waived because of Amara's job at the school. Recalling God's faithful provision in that season, Riaan shares, "We never had excess, but we never lacked."

After high school, he sold everything he had to travel to the United States to attend college. He left India with three hundred dollars in his pocket and incalculable idealism about the future awaiting him.

Thanks to a connection in Texas, Riaan landed in Austin and spent the next four years at the University of Texas. Upon graduation, he moved into the corporate world, earning rapid promotions with his natural entrepreneurial skills and strong work ethic. He was an American success story.

Meanwhile, it seemed as though every one of Riaan's family members and friends was eager to become his matchmaker. "Riaan, I finally found a great gal for you," his friend Ishaan declared one afternoon. As it turns out, Ishaan was right. Riaan met Priya on Monday, they were engaged the following Saturday, and they married four months later.

Riaan's corporate journey accelerated almost as quickly as his engagement and marriage. Priya, too, climbed the ladder of success as she attained advanced degrees in chemistry.

Riaan and Priya's financial success was almost unimaginable to their families back in India. The couple seemed to be living in the land of milk and honey, and their families celebrated their achievements. One rule is often true for families who escape a life of poverty: You never return.

But God began to stir in their hearts a desire to return to India. "We saw generations stuck in poverty, generations unable to get out of the cycle," Riaan shares. "We had witnessed both physical and spiritual poverty, and we knew there was something for us to do."

While Riaan's mother understood and supported this call and sacrifice, the couple's extended families—seeing Riaan and Priya's success in the United States—weren't as enthusiastic. "God has taken you out of India," they said. "Don't even consider coming back."

Still, the couple grew in clarity about their call to return. The Lord kept knocking on their hearts, and they sensed Him saying, "You've been blessed amazingly. What are you going to do with it?"

Remembering his childhood, Riaan knew how close he had come to living in a slum and falling into poverty. He reflected on the Lord's faithfulness in breaking through and changing his trajectory. He remembered his mother sacrificing an entire month's wages in gratitude for the ways God had blessed them. How could he not try to help others—even if it demanded sacrifice?

At the same time, God stirred in Priya's heart. While attending a missions conference in Amsterdam, she sensed a clear call to return to their home community.

"Our family thought we were crazy," Riaan reflects. "Everybody was shocked that we were thinking of coming back." It seemed illogical to exchange a life of comfort and prosperity to be surrounded by struggle and poverty, but Riaan and Priya trusted the One inviting them into the trade. "God gave us peace in this massive change."

A Bad Trade

In Jeremiah, God kept reminding His people they had made a bad trade. They held on to the Temple as a building and failed to honor the God who inhabited it. They held on to religious rites and neglected the significance behind them. They held on to power and privilege and let go of the only One with ultimate authority. In love with wooden idols, they were apathetic toward the Living God and the needs of their neighbors.[2]

In what is believed to be Jeremiah's first sermon, he delivers God's reminiscences of Israel.[3] "I remember how eager you were to please me as a young bride long ago, how you loved me and followed me even through the barren wilderness."[4] But as the sermon progresses, it's clear this passion for service and sacrifice has died. Jeremiah goes on to accuse the people because they "went after things that do not profit."[5] Comfort and ease replaced vibrancy of mission, and it was only through pain and exile that they would learn to let go of the fleeting things that didn't ultimately matter.

The Lord's indictment is clear: "My people have exchanged their glorious God for worthless idols!"[6] The New Testament says we cannot serve two masters.[7] It asks, "What will it profit a man if he gains the whole world and forfeits his soul?"[8] Yet in ancient Judah and still today, people regularly sacrifice the eternal on the altar of the temporal. We think of the parable of the rich young ruler, who faithfully observed the law but could not sacrifice what he believed would profit him most—his wealth.[9] How ironic that the very things we work so hard to acquire may be the things that cause us to walk away from what truly matters. To turn our back on God in favor of "things that do not profit."

In 2006, Riaan left his corporate life and its accompanying financial security. Shortly afterward, he and Priya sold their home and belongings—refusing to follow God's call halfheartedly—and relocated to India. The couple held on to what mattered most. Willing to let go of comfort and a life of stability, they courageously followed the Spirit's stirrings to return.

When Everything Goes Wrong

After sixteen years in the United States, attending college and working in corporate finance, Riaan was ready to apply his knowledge to his newly founded nonprofit to help families work their way out of poverty. His nonprofit model focused on economic and spiritual transformation through savings groups, which taught men and women to pool their own resources and make small loans to one another for emergency use or business investment. Studying the broad landscape of poverty interventions, he believed the combination of a job and the hope of Jesus was the best way to impact vulnerable communities. He knew loan sharks preyed on this same population, and over half of human trafficking was tied to debt.[10]

Riaan understood his mission, and his entrepreneurial experience in the U.S. had prepared him to launch and lead a nonprofit. But while he thought he knew the Indian culture of his youth, it didn't take long for Riaan to realize that his time away had created a cultural rift.

Inside the nonprofit, frustration grew among the nascent team. Riaan cared about deliverable results, and no one pushed back on the lofty goals he set. In India, junior employees rarely challenge a leader's vision. Riaan charged forward with a new leadership model without adjusting what had worked in the U.S. to this different culture and context. As a result, bitterness grew among a split staff.

Riaan noticed and worked to repair the damage. But even as the team collaboratively set goals and engaged in mentoring and discipleship to align expectations and address internal tensions, they faced growing external challenges from government leaders who questioned the spiritual aspects of their work. They began to better understand the significant risks and threats of addressing spiritual poverty under a hostile Hindu government.

The internal and external challenges were much more complex than Riaan had imagined when he launched his ministry in 2006. "The needs on the ground are significant. It can discourage you to see women and children who have been exploited and broken by poverty." He adds, "Most of the time, I love what I do, but there are days when it seems everything goes wrong."

On the most difficult days, Riaan remains focused on his original call, on the beautiful obligation he and Priya have to serve in India. "The people we serve are daily reminders of our mission. Any challenges we face in our life and leadership pale in comparison to what these communities face."

It's not just an unrelenting focus on their mission. Through prayer and Scripture-reading, they keep looking upward again and again to sustain their outward focus. Riaan notes that frustration and cynicism would choke his ability to accomplish his mission were he not filled with and empowered by the Holy Spirit. To that end, he takes monthly retreat days to meditate on the Word and pray. He describes it as spending time "working on the ministry rather than in the ministry," drawing close to God.

Ultimately, Riaan recognizes that no program or approach to poverty alleviation can ever fully transform a family. "Life change takes time and only happens by the power of the Spirit," he shares. As a result of their faithful service, Riaan and Priya have a front-row seat to God's rescue as they help families escape poverty and witness the freedom and transformation the gospel brings.

Releasing Power and Privilege

Despite successful career paths in the United States, Riaan and Priya followed God's leading out of power and privilege and into lives of sacrificial service. To the consternation of some family members, they abandoned the American dream and instead chose to invest in the dreams of vulnerable families.

In spending time with Riaan in India, it was evident that their sacrifice wasn't drudgery; it was full of joy. Why? They chose to hold on to God and let go of everything else.

For Judah, Israel, and us, it's easy to hold on to the wrong things—our safety, our privilege, and our comfort. The tighter we grasp these things, the harder it is to submit fully to our Savior. This robs us of the joy that comes from upward and outward service.

As I (Peter) walked through one of India's slums with Riaan—who has partnered with HOPE International for fifteen years, serving as a model of and mentor in sacrificial service—we entered a ten-by-ten-foot home, where the sun's rays on the metal roof heated the cramped living quarters like an oven. I was a puddle of sweat.

We listened as the family in the home shared about how they were saving for their future, avoiding the traps of loan sharks, and opening a small-scale tailoring business. As we listened to their story, I didn't get the sense that Riaan was thinking about the sacrifices he had made to be there.

Instead, he seemed fully at ease—his service undeniably rooted in love. Rather than conjuring enough resilience to grit it out, Riaan truly loved his community. Despite the ongoing challenges around him, he engaged without hurry, pointing families toward the God of lasting hope.

Application Questions

1. Why do you think it is challenging to embrace sacrifice?
2. Do you view sacrifice as an opportunity to grow in Christ's love? Why or why not?
3. Has someone in your life made a sacrifice for your benefit? If so, how did this impact you?
4. What sacrifices might God be asking you to make?
5. What could be holding you back from making these sacrifices?

CHAPTER 14
FORGIVENESS

Forgiveness is the key that unlocks the door of resentment and the handcuffs of hatred. It is a power that breaks the chains of bitterness and the shackles of selfishness.

—Corrie ten Boom[1]

When May Abboud Melki and her husband returned to their home in Beirut, Lebanon, in early August 2020, they weren't sure what they would find.

Just a day earlier, an explosion at the port of Beirut had killed over 200 people and injured 6,000 others. The explosion ripped through the city, decimating roads, businesses, and homes within a six-mile radius. For a country still reeling from the impact of COVID-19, government corruption, and a 55% poverty rate, it seemed the explosion couldn't have come at a worse time.

Mercifully, the Melkis had been traveling the day of the blast. But when they returned to their home of sixty years, it was in shambles. Chairs hurled across the room. Curtain rods knocked down. Walls pierced with debris. Floor littered with shards of glass.

Taking in the chaos around her, May, age seventy-eight, walked straight to her piano—a gift from her husband—and began to play "Auld Lang Syne." Within moments, the peaceful tune filled the home.

As family and friends gathered to clear glass and debris, one paused to record May playing music amid the utter destruction. The video—which has since gone viral—became "a symbol of hope and peace among all of the despair."[2]

Crisis upon Crisis

"Despair," May's son, Camille, tells us, is a fitting word—not just to describe the days after the historic explosion but to recount Lebanon's tumultuous history.

"From 1975 to today, everything I remember has to do with a crisis—whether a civil war, economic downturn, or refugee influx. From childhood until now, I cannot remember an economically and politically stable time in our country."

Camille was just eight years old when civil war broke out in Lebanon. Over the next fifteen years, warring militia groups overran and devastated the country.

Neighboring Syria sent over 30,000 soldiers to intervene—but in the process, they secured control of Lebanon's politics, economy, and media, stripping the country of its independence for nearly thirty years.[3]

By the time Camille reached college age, Syria was rapidly expanding its military occupation in Lebanon. They were accused of kidnapping Lebanese citizens, establishing detention centers to suppress dissenting voices, controlling the news, and stifling the public witness of Christians.[4] Reports suggest Syrians were responsible for the deaths of 100,000 Lebanese and the flight of about half a million people from the country.[5]

As tensions grew, Camille's parents implored him to leave the country, and he listened. Since the militia had overtaken most universities in Lebanon, Camille traveled to the United States to pursue a college education.

He spent his early adulthood in Anderson, Indiana, earning a degree in business management, but upon his graduation, Camille felt compelled to return home to work with his parents in their family import business. "People kept asking me why I chose to return to Lebanon," he says.

Why come back when others were so eager to leave? In the last hundred years—especially with a rise in internal conflicts—emigration from Lebanon has increased dramatically. Today, it's estimated that there are 4.5 million Lebanese living in-country and 15 million living abroad.[6]

Camille started supporting his parents in their family business, but soon a different call began to take shape. His church needed a volunteer youth pastor, and Camille stepped in. Within a year, the youth program expanded from 7 to 150 students—growing so rapidly that it surpassed the size of the church itself!

"Though my work in the family business was the breadwinner, youth ministry was my joy," Camille shares.

A Wedding to Remember

By the late 1980s, escalating tensions in Lebanon erupted into another war as the Lebanese prime minister and, later, the president-elect—believed to be a reunification candidate—were assassinated. Lebanese forces, incensed by the Syrian occupation, took up arms against the Syrian militia. Young Lebanese men were expected to be drafted, and underlying fears spread that this war would be even uglier than the ones before it.

Just a few days into the fighting, the Melki family business was completely destroyed, as was the apartment that Camille's parents had recently bought for him and his fiancée. Again, Camille's parents begged him to leave. Camille decided to do so on one condition: He and Hoda would first marry in Lebanon. The families agreed, and the couple moved up their wedding date five months and married at the Melkis' home. "Surely people were thinking that we were crazy—having a wedding when everyone else was having a funeral."

The day was unlike any other. Camille remembers snipers shooting and bombs exploding across the street. At one point, a stray bullet hit the family's large living room window, and it shattered. "How we survived that day is just amazing," Camille reflects.

The chaos didn't stop after the wedding. As the couple reached the airport for their flight to the States, Syrian soldiers arrested Camille, targeting him for his age and gender. Yet because Camille's uncle—who traveled with the couple to see them off—had a diplomatic passport, Camille was released and permitted a safe exit from Lebanon.

Worn and wearied, the newlyweds finally arrived back in Anderson, Indiana, and stayed with family friends for several months. While thankful for the reprieve, both Camille and Hoda couldn't shake the calling to return to Lebanon.

Just three months later they left their tranquil life in Indiana and boarded a flight home to the chaos they had escaped, knowing God had called them to work in Lebanon. Without a clue as to what they were supposed to do upon arrival, the Melkis obeyed.

A Call to Ministry

As they settled in, Camille and Hoda discovered a shared passion for youth ministry and invited twenty-five high school- and college-aged students to their home. "We asked one simple question: 'Where do you see yourself in five years?'"

The first fifteen students, without hesitation, declared that they would be living outside the country; another five said they'd be actively planning to leave. When they asked the final five students why they would choose to stay in Lebanon, the answer took them aback: "We don't have anywhere else to go or any other place to call a new home." If it wasn't already evident in their voices, utter hopelessness was written across their faces. Every single one dreamed of leaving Lebanon.

"There's nothing worse than feeling like a desperate Christian," Camille reflects. "When the devil fails to steal our salvation, he starts to attack our joy and hope. Then we begin to operate as defeated Christians, going from despair to despair."

From that moment, Camille and Hoda sensed a clear calling to work with the young men and women in Lebanon—not to persuade anyone to stay in the country, nor to condemn anyone who planned to leave, but to partner with those who chose to remain in a way that honored God. "It's not whether you choose to stay or choose to leave—it's about how you can be all that you can be in the orbit where God wants you."

The couple decided to enter full-time pastoral ministry, which meant a trip back to the States for Camille to earn his master's degree in divinity. This time the couple was fully confident that they were supposed to be in Lebanon for the long haul—so confident, in fact, that when Camille was interviewing for a youth pastor position during his schooling, he made the hiring committee commit to firing him the day he graduated.

"I didn't want any temptation to stay," he says frankly. "I told them we needed to sign a contract that the day I graduated would be the day I would return home." The committee agreed. And sure enough, after Camille received his degree—and his proverbial pink slip—the couple returned to Lebanon.

Their return came on the heels of some unexpected news. Camille's uncle had passed away suddenly. Influential in Lebanon, his uncle had founded churches, an orphanage, and a Bible school. His abrupt absence left a gaping hole in many leadership teams.

Learning of Camille's return, the board of the Bible school asked if Camille would serve as their dean. "I'm not a classroom guy," Camille admits. "I'd much prefer working in the field with people than feeling constrained to four walls." Nevertheless, he committed to the Bible school for one year.

One year turned into twelve, and throughout his leadership there—first as dean, then as president—Camille encouraged the students to think beyond books and theology to practical applications of their knowledge. Little did he realize how valuable this approach would be in the years to come.

Reframing Perspectives

"It's always been about building lifelong friendships and seeing how God could use us in Lebanon." As Camille reflected on his early years of ministry, he shared his passion for the next generation to, likewise, step forward into everything God was inviting them to.

Biennially, the Melkis rounded up a group of enthusiastic teenagers to attend the church's international youth convention. In the summer of 2006, Camille and Hoda led another one of these trips and traveled with their two daughters and a group of thirteen teenagers to Anaheim, California, for the conference.

While they were there, war broke out once again—this time between Israel and Hezbollah. Over the next month, Hezbollah fired thousands of rockets into Israel, and Israel retaliated forcefully. In just thirty-three days, Lebanon was left in utter destruction with $3.5 billion in damage done to the country's infrastructure.[7] Over 950,000 Lebanese fled from their homes, and 200,000 of them never returned.[8]

Just a year prior, the Syrian army had finally withdrawn from Lebanon after thirty years of occupation. It was the first time the country saw the economy gaining strength and free elections instituted. The Lebanese had just been learning to hope again when this war erupted. "The war in 2006 left the country of Lebanon in total hopelessness and the Church of Lebanon in total helplessness," Camille remembers.

Over 7,000 miles from home, Camille found himself in a similar state of helplessness. "Personally, it was a shock. It was one of the first major conflicts that Lebanon went through when I wasn't actually in the country." He grieved as he watched the news, thought about loved ones back home, and considered the future of the nation. Exasperated, Camille, like Habakkuk and Jeremiah, cried out to God.

"Every time things are starting to progress, every time hope is on the rise, another war breaks out or another crisis happens. Why, God? Why again?" As questions multiplied, Camille and Hoda searched for answers, turning to God for His guidance and their next steps. The Melkis reflected together on John's account of Jesus healing a blind man. Approaching the man, the disciples asked Jesus why he was born blind. Was he paying for his sins? His parents' sins? Jesus responded, "It was not because of his sins or his parents' sins. . . . This happened so the power of God could be seen in him."[9]

As soon as they read that passage, Camille was convicted. He'd wasted time asking God why all these injustices were happening without realizing that God didn't owe him any sort of justification. Put simply, *why* was the wrong question. Instead, the better question to

> **Why** was the wrong question. Instead, the better question to ask was **how**, then, Lord, in the midst of despair, will Your name be honored and glorified?

ask was *how*, then, Lord, in the midst of despair, will Your name be honored and glorified?

"Most of the time, when you ask the *why* question, God won't give you an answer. Should you try the *how* question," Camille says with a smile, "you better have a notebook and a pen, because the answer is very, very long."

As they started to ask God how they could partner in His work of restoration, the Melkis received the clarity they craved. With fresh vision, they packed up to return to Lebanon.

"When we told people we were headed back home to Lebanon, lots of people—including our own families—told us we were crazy." After all, the thirty-three-day war had prompted a frenzied mass exodus of people from the country. "People told us that if we weren't thinking of ourselves, we needed to think about our children. It's one thing to make the decision for yourself, but to be accused of not caring for your kids? That was tough."

"On the plane back to Lebanon, I asked my wife, 'Why do you think we're doing what we're doing?'"

"Because you're crazy," Hoda responded without hesitation.

Camille laughs as he recounts the conversation. "And I told her that I am and will continue to be."

But when he prodded further, she responded resolutely, "We're doing this because God has a heart for Lebanon."

Heart for Lebanon

With that conviction, Camille and Hoda returned to Lebanon on a mission to lead people from despair to hope. "We know that God's heart breaks and aches for every injustice around the world," Camille shares. "He wants us to be His hands and feet to love on people who have been marginalized and rejected, to be the voice of the voiceless, and to help the helpless."

Since asking God *how* they can partner with Him in bringing His love to Lebanon, the Melkis have seen the Holy Spirit answer and provide in tangible ways.

Their conviction became the name of their new nonprofit: Heart for Lebanon. Starting with no resources, the Melkis connected with their nascent team of volunteers every week. Together, the team pooled a few funds each Tuesday, put their collections toward ministry in southern Lebanon on Wednesday, and reconnected on Thursday. The question was always the same: Where did you see God at work?

In the beginning, the team replied dismally, "We've not seen God at work at all."

"What *have* you seen?" Camille prodded again.

"We've seen homes cleaned, schools rebuilt, basic needs met, and children happy—but nobody has prayed with us or accepted Christ as their Savior."

Camille recalled his years at the Bible school, stirring students to think beyond theology toward the practical application of their studies. He told the team, "Every home you've cleaned, every school you've helped to rebuild, every mattress you've given, every smile you've brought back, every prayer you've prayed, every beautiful message of hope you've shared has shown these people who Christ is."

Refugee Crises

Three years in, Heart for Lebanon's ministry was continuing to grow and flourish. Tensions remained high between Lebanon's pro-government groups and the Hezbollah-led opposition, yet the Heart for Lebanon team continued to move forward—partnering with God to rebuild cities and renew hope across the country.

"The only problem," Camille shares, "was that we thought the 2006 war was huge. We didn't realize the number of problems that would surface in the years to come."

In 2009, Iraqi refugees started to flood into Jordan, Syria, and Lebanon, seeking asylum after decades of war and violence in Iraq. The Human Rights Watch reported that 50,000 Iraqis settled in Lebanon that year. In response, the Heart for Lebanon team pivoted their focus to care for the large influx of people arriving at the country's eastern border.[10]

While the Iraqi refugee crisis was enormous, Camille admits, it was nothing compared to the Syrian refugee crisis two years later. When civil war broke out in neighboring Syria in 2011, the crisis displaced millions of people, most of whom poured into Lebanon.[11]

This refugee crisis was exponentially more difficult—not only because of the numbers but also because of recent history. The Syrians had occupied Lebanon for thirty years until 2005. "These were the people who shot at us, arrested us, killed our loved ones, destroyed our homes, and burned our businesses," Camille says. "We could connect with the Iraqi refugees—many of whom had come from Christian-persecuted communities—but working with Syrians was a whole different story."

That September, Heart for Lebanon hosted its annual staff retreat. Camille remembers his message well: "From the stage, I shared that we would not decrease our work with Iraqi refugees, but we were going to increase our work to care for and love the incoming Syrian refugees, too." He looked up from his notes to see each of his team members with the same expression on their faces: *Oh, we're not going to do that.*

"When we cannot forgive, we have to ask, 'Why is this?'" reflects Dickens Thunde, national director for World Vision International in Ghana. "We don't have the right to write off anyone. God gave us a second chance. How can we not do the same for those who wrong us?"[12]

The prospect of serving the Syrians was scary, Camille acknowledged. It brought up past wounds and horrific memories. Remembering his parents' home and the businesses that were destroyed, his arrest by Syrian soldiers, his daughter surviving a car bomb planted by Syrian fighters—Camille admitted that choosing to love the Syrian refugees was difficult and deeply personal. He knew that many of his team members carried physical and emotional scars from the Syrian occupation of Lebanon. Some might even be glad to see Syrians suffering.

Theologian Frederick Buechner writes of our propensity to cling to unforgiveness, "Of the Seven Deadly Sins, anger is possibly the most fun. To lick your wounds, to smack your lips over grievances long past, to roll over your tongue the prospect of bitter confrontations still to come, to savor to the last toothsome morsel both the pain you are given

Many didn't even know who Christ was. Some asked if He could stop by the next time He was in town so they could personally thank Him.

and the pain you are giving back—in many ways it is a feast fit for a king. The chief drawback is that what you are wolfing down is yourself. The skeleton at the feast is you."[13]

The team could not simultaneously nurture their grievances and love their neighbors. They could not allow unforgiveness to continue eating away at them. To press onward, they needed to look upward to the Source of forgiveness.

In the coming months, Camille watched as God infused the Heart for Lebanon team with His heart, with fresh love and forgiveness for the people they hated most.

"What takes us into a Syrian refugee tent settlement is not our naïveté, not financial, political, or personal gain," he shares. "There's nothing that brings us into the Syrian refugee settlement camps but Christ's love and forgiveness."

Every time the team members entered one of these camps, Syrians asked them why they were there. Was it to feel vindicated? To see—even celebrate—their suffering? The team answered the same way every time: "We're here to show you the love of Jesus Christ." To Camille's great surprise and sadness, many didn't even know who Christ was. Some asked if He could stop by the next time He was in town so they could personally thank Him.

Choosing to Forgive

In the middle of Jeremiah, after many chapters outlining the Israelites' offenses against God and one another, God gives His people a message of hope: a promise of restoration and redemption. "And I will forgive their wickedness," He declares, "and I will never again remember their sins."[14] Near the end of the book of Jeremiah, we're again encouraged by this message from the Lord: "In those days . . . no sin will be found in Israel or in Judah, for I will forgive the remnant I preserve."[15]

This echoes what Jeremiah wrote in Lamentations, "The faithful love of the LORD never ends! His mercies never cease. Great is his faithfulness; his mercies begin afresh each morning."[16]

Though the Israelites' greatest offenses were against God, they also relentlessly persecuted Jeremiah. Despite the people of Judah abusing him with mockery, threats, and confinement, Jeremiah continues to pray steadfastly for them. Although he cries out to God to repay their cruelty, he consistently intercedes on their behalf and pleads with them to abandon the destructive path they're pursuing.

Jeremiah emulated his forgiving Father. The One who, early in the book, asks the prophet to search for "a single soul who does what is right" for whose sake He could show mercy.[18] Even as the book of Jeremiah laments a broken covenant between God and His people, it looks forward to a new covenant in which our sins are forgiven. It foreshadows Jesus' dying request: "Father, forgive them."[19]

The more we look up and understand this radical gift of mercy and forgiveness, the more we will be able to extend it to others. Leaders who last have learned how to extend forgiveness.

Because his roots in Christ were deep, Camille could look at the Syrian refugee crisis—remembering all that he and his family suffered at the hands of Syrian soldiers during the occupation of Lebanon—and commit to forgive, love, and serve the Syrian people. God's forgiveness compelled Camille and the Heart for Lebanon team to forgive the very people who had committed atrocities against them.

Forgive Us

While Camille's story emphasizes the importance of extending forgiveness to others, there is the parallel invitation to seek forgiveness when we have been the offender. Jesus paired the ideas of giving and receiving forgiveness when He taught His disciples to pray, "Forgive us our sins, as we have forgiven those who sin against us."[20]

In Matthew 5:23–24, He gives clear instructions for those who realize they have wronged another: "If you are presenting a sacrifice at the altar in the Temple and you suddenly remember that someone has something against you, leave your sacrifice there at the altar. Go and be reconciled to that person. Then come and offer your sacrifice to God."

If in the course of our worship, or our Kingdom-expanding work, we realize we have wronged someone, God charges us to immediately initiate a process of reconciliation and restoration. We may be called to pastor a church or lead a ministry, but more fundamentally we are called to be "Christ's ambassadors:"[21] to represent Him well. One way we do that is by admitting when we haven't.

It's deeply humbling to confess that our actions or inaction has harmed another. That we have fallen short, offered a distorted reflection of our God, and hurt each other—with or without intention. But in these inevitable moments, the most powerful thing we can do, for ourselves and for a watching world, is to humbly seek forgiveness.

We long for God's grace to flow within and out from the Church as we become a community of people who give and receive abundant forgiveness.

Signs of Hope

Over the past decade, Camille's team has had ample opportunity to give and receive forgiveness as 1.5 million Syrian refugees have fled to Lebanon, the largest per capita host of refugees worldwide.[22] The Heart for Lebanon team has served tens of thousands of Syrian refugees, many of whom now serve as staff on their team alongside Iraqis, Lebanese, Egyptians, and more. Camille calls it a "beautiful mosaic."

Heart for Lebanon's mission hasn't changed. They continue to lead people from despair to hope by providing Lebanon's most marginalized citizens and refugees with physical necessities such as food and bedding, faith-based education for children, and a relational support system. They continue to press onward in forgiveness and faith.

That's not to say it's grown easy. "Every time we think it cannot get any worse, it gets worse," Camille shares. Like the prophet Jeremiah experienced thousands of years earlier, pain is part of the journey. And sometimes, just when you think it can't get any worse . . . it does.

With the most recent wave of challenges facing Lebanon, Camille continues, "The world has crumbled under COVID-19, but the pandemic is only one problem of many that Lebanon is facing." In addition to the blast that annihilated his parents' home and cost the country $12 billion in damages, Camille referenced political turbulence, economic desperation, and the ongoing refugee influx facing Lebanon.

Yet, after each crisis, his message to the staff is the same: "Our call has not changed. We are going to continue to care for every opportunity God gives us to serve."

We might wonder what compels a person like Camille—who has the opportunity to flee with his wife and children—to stay and work in a country bombarded with crises.

Camille says the answer is found in the question he asks of God every morning: "Amid all the despair around me, could You give me one sign of hope today?"

And every day, without exception, hope shows up and prompts him to get to work.

Some days it's found in the love offerings given by Syrian refugees—who've come with just the clothes on their backs—to help the Lebanese communities and churches rebuild after the explosion.

Some days it's found in the calls from former students who have since emigrated from Lebanon, asking how they can help other students who are facing great financial need.

Some days it's found in the face of an Iraqi immigrant who donates his first, very meager paycheck to help rebuild the home of his Lebanese neighbor.

And some days it's found amid the chaos, among the shards of glass and debris littering a home, and a mother sitting at her piano, playing the soft, peaceful strains of "Auld Lang Syne"—a beautiful reminder that God is nearer than we think.

Application Questions

1. Do you tend to ask God, "Why is this happening?" How might asking, "How will Your name be honored and glorified in the midst of this happening?" change your perspective?

2. How have the mercy, forgiveness, and love of Christ changed your life?

3. Who might you consider your "enemies"? Are there people who have hurt or offended you?

4. If "leaders who last have learned how to extend forgiveness," would you consider yourself someone who has made this choice? Why or why not?

5. What does it look like to love your enemies with Christ's love?

CHAPTER 15
ONWARD

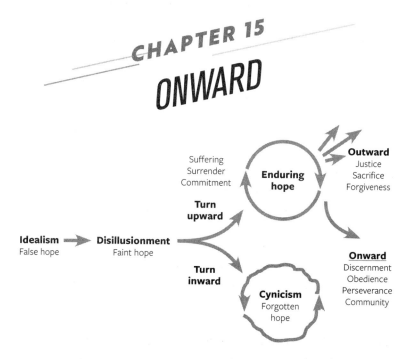

We can rejoice, too, when we run into problems and trials, for we know that they help us develop endurance. And endurance develops strength of character, and character strengthens our confident hope of salvation. And this hope will not lead to disappointment. For we know how dearly God loves us, because he has given us the Holy Spirit to fill our hearts with his love.

—Romans 5:3–5

When we began learning from the leaders profiled in this book, we had only a loose working theory of the connection between hope and long-term service. But in our conversations with these leaders, parallel themes consistently emerged, and our thesis began to grow clear. The first, and perhaps most obvious, theme was their shared love for Jesus. They looked upward to the One who sustains their service. The second was their outward focus and commitment to loving their neighbors. And the third was something few would strive for: their long-suffering. What a terrible word: *long + suffering*! We're inclined to prefer short-suffering, momentary-suffering—or best of all—no-suffering.

Yet God's presence and power was so evident in these leaders' lives in the way they responded to a host of terribly difficult circumstances. Still more noteworthy was how many of these long-suffering leaders have served the very people who contributed to their suffering.

These leaders model what it looks like to turn upward, then outward, and finally press onward. Despite wounds and scars, they retain an unflagging commitment to long-term service. They are, as the apostle Paul urged the Corinthians to be, "steadfast, immovable, always abounding in the work of the Lord, knowing that in the Lord [their] labor is not in vain."[1] Enduring hope, rooted in faith, produces patience. It expands timelines. Paul modeled this perspective perhaps better than anyone else. Amid disappointment, heartache, and persecution, he wrote that "our light and momentary troubles are achieving for us an eternal glory that far outweighs them all."[2]

How could Paul call his experiences "light and momentary"? We know he had a thorn in the flesh, presumed to be with him for the entirety of his life.[3] He was accustomed to "afflictions, hardships, calamities, beatings, imprisonments, riots, labors, sleepless nights, [and] hunger."[4] There's nothing light nor momentary about his circumstances. And there's nothing that feels light or momentary when we're addressing seemingly intractable obstacles today.

Paul explains his perspective: "So we don't look at the troubles we can see now; rather, we fix our gaze on things that cannot be seen. For the things we see now will soon be gone, but the things we cannot see will last forever."[5]

Paul reminds us that we must turn upward to continue pressing onward. A glimpse of God extends our timeline and shifts our perspective.

Likewise, Jeremiah, The Persevering Prophet, began his ministry with a glimpse of God. In Jeremiah 1:19, the prophet receives God's assurance: "They will fight against you, but they shall not prevail against you, for I am with you, declares the Lord, to deliver you" (ESV). Jeremiah knew that despite dire circumstances, he could trust God's promised presence.

In Lamentations 3, Jeremiah writes, "The Lord is good to those who wait for him, to the soul who seeks him."[6] Waiting is expected, and we are invited into a patient posture.

U.S. Navy Vice Admiral James Stockdale understood the difficulty of holding on to hope and the importance of extending our timelines. As a prisoner of war in Vietnam, he faced a brutal present—with regular abuse and torture—and an unknown future. Despite this, he sought to lead and inspire his fellow prisoners, offering steadfast hope in a situation that grew bleaker by the day.

When reflecting on his experience, he remembers that the prisoners who "felt they would be 'home by Christmas' fared much worse

> He came to realize the importance of an informed optimism: the hope of an eventual escape with a realistic perspective on just how long and difficult that might be.

mentally than those who understood it might take much longer and adjusted." He came to realize the importance of an informed optimism: the hope of an eventual escape with a realistic perspective on just how long and difficult that might be. Named after him, "The Stockdale Paradox" is based on his experience and further social science research on the power of informed hopefulness.[7]

Whether in prison or facing complex leadership challenges, we're reminded that extending our timelines with informed optimism helps us to press on too.

To last, we need to adjust our expectations of how long and difficult this work will be. It will be a far more arduous climb than we can imagine, but we can anchor our optimism in the reality of God's presence and promise to be *with* us, up to and including a final chapter that is better than we could dare to imagine.

Leaders who last turn upward, they turn outward, and they walk onward. We see this in leaders who discern God's call in Zambia (chapter 16), obediently address inequality in Detroit (chapter 17), persevere in exhorting the Church to be a faithful witness in the Philippines (chapter 18), and build a strong community to sustain service in Poland (chapter 19). Through difficulties and disappointments, each demonstrates why long + suffering might not be such a bad thing after all.

Application Questions

1. Knowing God can work through suffering, where can you invite Him to develop character and bring enduring hope into your life?

2. What are you committed to long term? How do you see suffering playing a role in that long-term commitment?

3. When you consider your life in 5, 10, 20, or 40 years, what is your objective? Where is your focus?

4. How might your life change if you viewed suffering as "light and momentary afflictions"?

CHAPTER 16
DISCERNMENT

The purpose of God is not to answer our prayers, but by our prayers we come to discern the mind of God.

—Oswald Chambers[1]

While Dr. Phil Thuma has spent most of his life combatting the malaria epidemic, he spent his early years coming face-to-face with another debilitating disease: apartheid.

In the second half of the twentieth century, apartheid—meaning "apartness" in Afrikaans—was legalized in South Africa and neighboring Zambia.[2] A system of racial segregation, apartheid controlled and impoverished non-white Africans for close to fifty years, forcing them to live in separate areas and use different public facilities from white citizens; limiting job prospects and access to health care; and reinforcing separation through unequal education. The racial hierarchy of apartheid left gaping wounds, comparable to the persistent effects of the abolished caste system in India and the systemic racial hierarchy in the post–Civil War United States.

In the 1950s and '60s, Christian missionaries—who had come primarily from the United States and Europe—were raising their white children in places like Zambia, preaching a Christian message of God's love for all while often reinforcing or accepting the oppressive system of apartheid. "Missionaries and other white Christians were alarmed by the idea that the equality of all people before God means they should be equal in public life," writes Richard H. Elphick, author of *The Equality of Believers*, a book about Protestant missionaries in neighboring South Africa.[3]

Also writing of South Africa, Neville Richardson, former associate professor of theological ethics at the University of KwaZulu-Natal, South Africa, writes:

> The church under apartheid was polarized between "the church of the oppressor" and "the church of the oppressed." Either you were for apartheid or you were against it; there was no neutral ground. Given the heavy-handed domination of the minority white government, those who imagined themselves to be neutral were, unwittingly perhaps, on the side of apartheid. This complicity was especially true of those Christians who piously "avoided politics" yet enjoyed the social and economic benefits of the apartheid system.[4]

Phil was just four years old when his family moved to Macha—an isolated, rural community in southern Zambia—to build a hospital and serve as missionaries. Yet even in this missionary community, Phil recognized racism in many of the missionaries with whom his family served. "Growing up as a missionary kid, I could see the negatives and the positives—and there were more negatives than positives," he recalls.

Rather than working against the ugly injustice of apartheid, the missionaries Phil observed in Zambia largely acquiesced to the prevailing cultural trend, which socially and economically oppressed those they purported to serve. Although these individuals continued on as missionaries, their lack of discernment on this single issue hampered their witness and undermined their efforts to faithfully serve and act as Christ's ambassadors in Zambia.

The Church's hypocrisy wasn't a source of disillusionment for Phil alone; many others also walked away from faith and service because of the oppressive legacies missionaries themselves had left.

A Faith of His Own

After finishing high school in Zambia, Phil returned to the United States to pursue further education and embark on the next phase of his life. As he wrestled with his personal beliefs about God, he was sure of only one thing: He would *never* be a missionary.

Instead, he enrolled in medical school and assumed various internships and positions in the medical field with plans to become a family practitioner, an internist, or a surgeon. Despite early reservations about and rebellions against Christianity, Phil sensed a shift in his life during his early married years, as he was able to differentiate Jesus from the negative examples of those who claimed to be His followers but participated in apartheid.

As he and his wife, Elaine, became more involved in their local church, Phil heard that Macha, Zambia—the very community where he had grown up—needed a doctor to fill a two-year term. While he didn't think of himself as a missionary, Phil liked the idea of introducing his family to a place that had been so formative in his own life. His wife, a nurse, also liked the idea and embraced this short-term adventure.

Over the next two years, the Thumas volunteered with Brethren in Christ World Missions and were assigned to work at the two-hundred-bed Macha Mission Hospital. Phil served as one of the two doctors at the hospital, and Elaine volunteered as a nurse. During their service, they attended the Brethren in Christ church in Macha.[5]

Toward the end of their second year in Macha, Phil grew restless. He felt strongly that God had called them to Zambia for two years of voluntary service, but those two years were almost up—and he didn't know what was next. As Phil struggled to discern next steps, a local Zambian church leader asked him to share a sermon for a youth conference, and Phil chose to preach on finding God's will.

Preparing that sermon became a defining moment for Phil.

"To this day, I can tell you where I was sitting and what I was doing when it hit me: I knew that I needed to work in Zambia as a full-time missionary and as a pediatrician—two of the things I'd sworn never to do." Phil recalls that moment as the closest he's come to hearing the audible voice of the Lord.

In those days, most long-term medical missionaries were told to train as surgeons. But as Phil—a self-proclaimed "data nut"—looked at the numbers, he recognized that the highest mortality rate in Macha was with children, who were often dying of malaria, a disease that was largely obsolete—and treatable—in other parts of the world. It was as if the data was confirming God's word to him about missionary pediatrics.

Phil and Elaine returned to the States so he could begin training as a pediatrician. He completed his pediatric residency at Johns Hopkins Children's Center, one of the most prestigious pediatric hospitals in the country. A few years later, the family returned to Macha, where Phil went on to lead the Macha Mission Hospital that his dad helped to build.

Malaria on the Rise

By the late 1980s, malaria was taking sub-Saharan Africa by storm. A parasitic disease spread by the bites of infected mosquitoes, malaria affected 300–500 million people and killed over a million each year.[6] A mosquito injects 10–100 parasites into its victim. As the parasites develop and multiply in the liver and subsequently in red blood cells, the result can be up to 250 *billion* parasites in a person's bloodstream.[7] While malaria symptoms—notably a high fever and chills—could begin within weeks of infection, the parasites could lie dormant in the body for up to a year.

Worse, these parasites developed resistance to the main forms of medication available in the 1980s, making effective treatment nearly impossible.

In 1988, malaria killed more and more children in sub-Saharan Africa, with close to 3,000 children under the age of five dying *every day*.[8] And Macha, where Phil worked, became a breeding ground for the disease. Cases had more than doubled among in-patients and more than tripled among outpatients.

Phil shares, "I had been trying to be the best doctor I could be for these kids, but we were working day and night to take care of those with severe malaria and watching many die. Even three weeks prior, many of the children had been healthy and strong."

"I remember my own bouts with malaria," says Chilobe Kalambo, a HOPE International board member who grew up near the hospital in Macha. "I remember the almost daily, distinct sound of deep grief I used to hear emanating from wailing parents as they carried their dead children one last time from the pediatric ward to the mortuary."

The epidemic became personal for Phil and his family. His own children developed serious symptoms. "Every day I'd watch kids die from malaria in the hospital. Then I'd come home to hear my wife say that one of our kids had a positive malaria scare that day. I couldn't help but think, 'Will they be next?'"

New Treatment

After several years of missionary service in Zambia, the Thuma family moved back to the United States to comply with policies established by their missions agency. Phil landed a job in the pediatric department at Penn State University, where he continued his malaria research, traveling to Zambia regularly and continuing to run projects in Macha.

Around this time, the World Health Organization (WHO) released an update on a new malaria drug ready to be tested in humans. This was the news Phil had been waiting for, and he put in a bid to test the new treatment in Macha. To his surprise, WHO accepted the bid, selecting Macha as one of three African communities in which to conduct the new drug tests.

WHO representatives traveled to Macha to meet with Phil and his research team. After obtaining ethical approval, the team began treating malaria-positive community members with the new drug. They tested recipients' blood every four to six hours, counting the parasites under a microscope. Whereas previously the parasites would leave slowly, only to return, the new drug made the parasites disappear rapidly. After decades of research, experiments, and tests, the world had finally uncovered a new treatment for malaria—and *it worked*!

The drug needed to undergo a series of rigorous tests and trials in the coming years until it was proved safe and effective for widespread use.

The process took ten agonizing years.

During this decade, while living in the United States, Phil attended diligently to his research and presented about the new drug at international conferences. But his work-sponsored trips to Macha were gut-wrenching as he tried caring for malaria patients with the less effective, available medications. He couldn't bear to watch children die, knowing there was a much better drug simply awaiting approval.

He sensed God's call to resign from his position at Penn State University in order to pursue full-time malaria research. Since he was only a year out from becoming a full professor, Phil's decision to quit his well-paying job didn't make financial sense. The department chair accused him of having a midlife crisis. But as Henri Nouwen wrote, "Discernment is a life of listening to a deeper sound and marching to a different beat, a life in which we become 'all ears.'"[9]

And Phil knew whose voice he must follow.

After an ongoing discernment process that included prayer and seeking counsel from friends and family, Phil decided to start a nonprofit in the basement of his home in Dillsburg, Pennsylvania. The nonprofit would allow him to devote full-time work to malaria research, writing grants to eradicate malaria and serve children in Macha. To support the new endeavor, he and his family sold their second car and remortgaged their home.

"My goal was to use my ability and knowledge to make sure those children had a chance," Phil shares.

Resistance to the Mission

As Phil started writing grants on behalf of the Macha community, he grappled with the enormity of the epidemic. It was well-known that malaria had never been controlled in Zambia, and people regularly reminded Phil of that fact. Cynics had plenty of evidence and ammunition with which to attack him.

You're crazy. Malaria is just too big. You'll never be able to secure grants for malaria research—from your basement, no less!

But Phil kept looking upward to follow God's leading, and he kept focusing outward as well. His discernment of God's call on his life, combined with his love for the people of Macha, convinced him to press on. He believed children shouldn't be left to die from a preventable disease simply because of where they were born.

Johns Hopkins School of Public Health—a part of Johns Hopkins University, where Phil had studied pediatrics—received a large grant to open a malaria research institute. They wanted not only to treat malaria but also to study the disease with the eventual goal of eradication. They'd work with mosquitoes directly, genetically modifying the insects for malaria resistance with the idea of reintroducing them into a community to reproduce. Johns Hopkins was looking for a field station in a malaria-endemic country, and Phil negotiated with them for a grant to build the infrastructure in Macha.

Plans developed quickly. Yet as soon as the Zambian government learned a U.S. institution planned to invest a bunch of money "in the bush," they firmly blocked it, demanding the research site be built instead in Lusaka, Zambia's capital. Johns Hopkins, interested in working where malaria was most rampant, stood their ground—and the plans came to a grinding halt.

The setback brought Phil to a crossroads, threatening his hopefulness about this new venture he thought God had so clearly called him to pursue. Again he reached the pivot point of disillusionment.

"I got discouraged," Phil says. "I'd worked all my life to reach this wonderful opportunity to work with a well-known group of scientists who were willing to invest time, funds, and resources to make a difference in the Macha community—and then it was blocked by the government."

God and King

Many authorities vied for a voice in Phil's call: from Zambian government leaders to well-meaning colleagues to friends who wanted to spare him the pain of seemingly inevitable failure. If he had followed their advice, Macha might look very different today, and Phil would have missed the opportunity to be a part of God's miraculous work of transformation in that community. Though the noise of other opinions could be loud, Phil tuned his heart to God's voice, pursuing a path quite distinct from that of the Israelites in the era of kings.

For a time, God himself was Israel's King. When the Israelites ask the prophet Samuel to appoint a king to lead them, it comes as a personal rejection against God as their king. God knows that following an at-best-imperfect follower would distance His people from Him. He tells Samuel to warn the people what a king will demand from them: their children for battle; their labor for his glory and profit; their land, flocks, and harvest to reward his favored few.

The people continue undeterred in their single-minded, reckless pursuit of a king. And the Lord tells Samuel to give them what they've asked for.[10] Given the choice between being led by their faithful God or a fallible man, the Israelites chose to put their trust in a man.

Saul was the first of many kings who would lead the nation imperfectly, some more and some less faithful to their God. In Jeremiah 22, the prophet addresses King Jehoiakim, who falls into the latter category. "Be fair-minded and just. Do what is right!" the prophet implores. "If you refuse to pay attention to this warning . . . this palace will become a pile of rubble."[11]

We're left to imagine how much time has elapsed, but by the end of the chapter, God has declared His judgment: "[Jehoiachin, son of Jehoiakim] is a failure, for none of his children will succeed him on the throne of David to rule over Judah."[12] Peterson's *The Message* captures the full implication of God's pronouncement: "He's the end of the line, the last of the kings."[13]

The Babylonians deported Jehoiachin and installed in his place a regent, Zedekiah, who had pledged an oath of allegiance to Nebuchadnezzar. After centuries of unfaithful service to their King, Israel's kings were no more.

For anyone whose faith was in an earthly empire, this was terrible news. But with this pronouncement of judgment came a promise. The next chapter of Jeremiah is among the most hope-filled in the book.

God pronounces judgment on those who have led astray his "sheep" (creatures not known for their discerning ways) but vows that He will personally gather His flock.[14] He gives them another chance to pursue His leadership. To discern His voice. Alluding to Christ, He promises to "raise up a righteous descendant from King David's line. He will be a King who rules with wisdom. He will do what is just and right throughout the land."[15]

How often we look for someone to lead us—whether it's the kings of Old Testament days, missionaries who came before, or "celebrity" church leaders. All will follow imperfectly. All will disappoint. But we're invited to be led by the true King. In Jeremiah 31, God outlines a new covenant for His people.

> "I will put my instructions deep within them,
>   and I will write them on their hearts.
> I will be their God,
>   and they will be my people.
> And they will not need to teach their neighbors,
>   nor will they need to teach their relatives, saying, 'You should
>   know the LORD.'
> For everyone, from the least to the greatest,
>   will know me already."[16]

We are invited to *know* God. To discern His will and seek His grander vision. To quit following kings who will lead us astray and instead devote ourselves to our true King, who leads us onward in love and outward in service.

Establishing the Macha Research Trust

Despite his disappointment over the deadlock between the Zambian government and the Johns Hopkins investors, Phil chose hope. He remembered God's call to pursue this work. He framed this denial as an opportunity to get to know the leaders in the Zambian government. Refusing to become a cynic, Phil regularly met with leaders in Lusaka, demonstrating through the data why Macha was the right place to build a research institute.

Eventually the unsupportive government leaders left office. When new leaders arrived, they gave Phil and the Johns Hopkins team the green light to work in Macha.

After years of disappointment, Phil and the team finally established the Malaria Institute at Macha (MIAM) in the early 2000s, which later became known as the Macha Research Trust (MRT). The Trust, built in collaboration with Johns Hopkins School of Public Health and the

We are invited to **know** God. To discern His will and seek His grander vision. To quit following kings who will lead us astray and instead devote ourselves to our true King, who leads us onward in love and service.

Macha Mission Hospital, included a research field station and training center to continue malaria research directly in the field. From the beginning, Phil knew the importance of local leadership and vision, a realization spurred by his early disillusionment with top-down missionary efforts.

He saw this as an opportunity to build not only physical but also intellectual infrastructure. He believed in Zambians' leadership capacity and lamented the way previous colonial missionary work and health initiatives had relied on foreign expertise and even actively discouraged local leadership. Phil took a different approach. He hired capable Zambians—many of whom were subsistence farmers—and invested in their capacity. Over time, they grew to become leading global researchers.

Early management meetings focused on listening to community members as they shared their needs and priorities. This was not going to be a foreign project or solution; this was a homegrown initiative with collective ownership of the vision.

As the MRT started to grow, the team received long-awaited good news: The anti-malaria medicine Coartem had finally been approved for widespread use. With just a few minor side effects, this medicine proved incredibly effective against malaria.

Around the same time, rapid diagnostic tests replaced microscope counts. These advances in testing methodology empowered the MRT team to visit villages and test people for malaria on the spot. If villagers tested positive, Phil and his team could deliver the much-needed Coartem right away.

Long-Term Commitment

While the prevailing narrative at the time was that malaria could not be controlled in Africa, a different story unfolded in Macha. Global malaria experts visited the rural Zambian community just to see if the rumors were true.

The evidence was undeniable: Malaria in Macha was on the decline. Between 2000 and 2019, malaria deaths in children under age five decreased by more than 95% in the area.[17] Tens of thousands of children survived into adulthood because of the work of Phil and his partners at MRT.

It was the miracle in Macha, as it became the first region in Africa to almost completely eliminate malaria.[18]

Many international scientists work in a place like Macha for a season. Few devote their entire working life to a single location. But Phil's singular commitment has opened doors to share his respect for his dedicated Zambian colleagues—as well as his God-given vision for what could be accomplished in Macha by honoring and honing local capacity.

As scientists, researchers, Ph.D. students, and doctors visit Macha today, they immerse themselves in the mission. They learn, work, and pray together with the MRT team, who routinely share the motivation behind their work and why they're drawn to stay. The Zambian team is influencing global health and expanding the borders of what is considered possible—even while expanding the Kingdom.

Today, the MRT has published over one hundred scientific articles. Their institute is built on Christ's love and their belief that science and Christianity are not in conflict but in harmony.

Phil continues to engage in as much research as possible in the Macha community. He loves investing in the local leaders, who ensure the longevity of the research and mission, extending Macha's positive outcomes to communities well beyond their borders.

When I (Peter) visited Macha in 2018, I saw netted areas full of mosquitoes used in tests and treatments.

"Are all those mosquitoes infected with malaria?" I asked while pointing to a netted area.

"Yes!" came the reply, prompting me to take a step back from the insects.

"But these are the only mosquitoes in our region that have malaria. They are inside the nets. Not outside," the researcher explained.

In this region, they've virtually defeated malaria. Kids no longer die from a bug bite. Children and their parents have hope for a malaria-free future.

Follow the Leader

After decades fighting malaria, Phil humbly summarizes his service, "We're simply called to use the abilities and brains God gave us for His glory." But Phil's long obedience, hope-filled vision, and faithful service almost didn't get off the ground.

For a season in his young adult life, cynicism gripped Phil's heart. He wanted no part in missionary service after witnessing the Church's complicity in colonial and apartheid abuses. But as Phil continued to mature in his faith, God gave him discernment, enabling him to disentangle Jesus' message from the example of those who followed Him imperfectly.

God called Phil not to toss aside the idea of missionary service—or even faith more broadly—but to work to remedy painful legacies and serve in a way that honored the capacity and worth of all people. In the words of 1 Thessalonians 5:21–22, the gift of discernment empowered

Phil to "hold on to what is good" while rejecting "every kind of evil." Phil knew that he, too, would not always get it right, yet that was no reason to cynically opt out of service. God was still moving in Macha and inviting him to restore physical health while pointing to the Restorer. And God equipped him with the ability not only to practice medicine but also to practice discernment.

Discernment remains vital in the lives of leaders who seek to press onward into long obedience and faithful service. It helps us critically evaluate and distinguish the helpful from the harmful, the true from the false, the good from the bad, in our own approaches and in others'. We cannot simply look inward and follow our hearts. As Jeremiah says, "The human heart is the most deceitful of all things, and desperately wicked. Who really knows how bad it is?"[19]

Nor can we place our ultimate trust in the wisdom or authority of other leaders. Instead, each leader must "learn to know God's will for you, which is good and pleasing and perfect,"[20] asking God for wisdom, which He has promised to give generously.[21]

As we see throughout the Old Testament, in the book of Jeremiah, and through Phil's example, the gift of discernment helps us distinguish the leading of our true King from that of lesser kings.

Application Questions

1. What or who do you tend to look to for wisdom instead of God? Why?

2. Can you recall a time in your life when you were led astray by following someone or something other than God?

3. Can you recall a time when you could discern the will of God and decided to follow it? How did this impact you?

4. What can you do to gain a greater awareness of God's voice in your life?

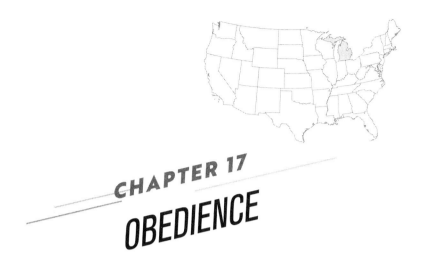

CHAPTER 17

OBEDIENCE

We delight in the Lord when we genuinely want His will more than our own will.

—Terry Looper[1]

The morning we spoke to Lisa Johanon, executive director of Central Detroit Christian Community Development Corporation (CDC), she had just dropped off cookies for a family new to her neighborhood. Though the gesture might imply a close-knit cul-de-sac community or a suburban housing development, the "neighborhood" she spoke of is at the heart of Detroit's city center.

"Detroit has been a racially and economically divided city for decades," Lisa summarizes. "Healing this divide takes time, presence, mutual trust, love, and prayer."[2] Hers is a "ministry of being present." Whether baking a casserole for a family experiencing loss, sitting with a lonely neighbor, or launching a new business to provide farm-fresh produce in a food desert, Lisa does it all to build community, promote peace, and bring the love of Jesus Christ to her neighbors in a challenging context.

Lisa lives and works in one of the poorest zip codes in the state of Michigan: 66% of her neighbors are unemployed, and 40% of residents earn less than $10,000 a year. More people are in wheelchairs from gunshot wounds here than anywhere else in the state, 42% of adults did not graduate from high school, and with only 4% of third graders reading on grade level, the future could seem less than brimming with possibility.[3]

Yet criticism of the neighborhood rankles Lisa. Statistics aside, central Detroit is the only home her two children—now in their twenties—have ever known, and she's fiercely protective of it. Lisa loves her home enough to work every day toward the restoration of not only the buildings but also the people surrounding her.

CDC invests in the people of central Detroit through education and employment assistance. They provide tutoring, financial literacy classes, and job readiness training. They serve meals, plant community gardens, and fill dumpsters with debris.

Since 50% of Lisa's neighbors have no car, interventions—including the provisions of nutritious food, safe housing, medical care, churches, and jobs—need to be *in the community* to be of any help. In response to this need, CDC invests in infrastructure such as affordable housing, a laundromat, and even a medical clinic.

CDC's dedicated staff members don't stop investing at the end of the workday. Like Lisa, CDC's twenty or so staff members live among the people they serve. The residency requirement is perhaps not CDC's most popular policy. Some well-qualified would-be employees are turned off by Lisa's insistence that they live within the two-mile-diameter territory served by CDC. But to Lisa, who relocated to central Detroit with her husband three decades ago, loving their neighbors means living among their neighbors. There's no option to "helicopter in and helicopter out."

Lisa's unapologetic about her high expectations. "Do you have to count the cost? Yeah," she states matter-of-factly. "But don't you want people in the trenches with you who have counted that cost?"

It's clear Lisa has had the opportunity to count and count again over the past three decades of long obedience: When the Great Recession swept away almost two decades of progress. When her home was robbed. When her son was stabbed. When her daughter—by Lisa's assessment a "third culture kid"—felt there was no place she truly belonged. Lisa feels called to obedience, not romanticism. The path has not been easy, but, "I know in the end, God wins. That's what keeps me going," she says. Turning upward, she continues to press onward despite the cost.

Growing up in Detroit's relatively affluent suburbs, Lisa's first significant exposure to poverty didn't come until, as a college student in Chicago, she encountered the infamous Cabrini-Green housing projects. What began in the 1940s as a much-lauded effort to address substandard housing for black and brown people had deteriorated, becoming—by the time Lisa arrived—a hub for drugs, gang activity, and weapons trafficking.

The once sought-after homes were synonymous with slum living: unclean, unsafe, and to Lisa, deeply unfair. "It was just appalling to me," she remembers. It was a place where the ugliness of institutionalized racism could be seen, felt, and even smelled. Instead of shaking her head and turning her back, Lisa was drawn into closer proximity. "We engaged in a lot of work there," she says, recalling the youth ministry that evolved into a church plant.

A "Strategic" Location

With justice at the forefront of her mind, Lisa pursued a law degree. She had not yet completed her coursework when she and her husband, a fellow graduate of Moody Bible Institute, felt called home to Detroit. But it wasn't the suburbs where Lisa was raised that beckoned the newlyweds. It was the city. Moving before finishing law school meant that Lisa would have to commute four-and-a-half hours one way to finish the program, yet the call felt too pressing to postpone.

The city seemed a world away from Lisa's childhood home. Knowing little of the area, Lisa and her husband took a map and plotted the midpoint between the two Youth for Christ offices she would oversee, with the aim of easy accessibility for her team.

Without researching demographics, schools, or crime rates, they bought a charming century-old home with original woodwork and a built-in fireplace for $29,000.⁴ The decision felt strategic. They didn't know they had just chosen the poorest zip code in the state of Michigan. "I was clueless about the challenges initially," she recollects.

Lisa led Bible studies and ministered to Detroit's young people as a Youth for Christ staff member. Meanwhile, she and her husband celebrated the birth of a son, and almost two years later, a daughter. They were putting down roots in their central Detroit neighborhood, and by the time Youth for Christ decided to close their Detroit offices after seven years of ministry in the city, it was already home.

Lisa describes what came next as a "wilderness season." She was the mother of two children under two. Since her daughter's birth, she had felt unwell, visiting the hospital at least monthly for diagnostic testing. Still, a diagnosis evaded Lisa for nine months—that is, until her doctors discovered a surgical error.

She lived in a city close to family and friends—many of whom lived in suburbs just ten miles away—yet they did not visit because of what Lisa describes as an "imaginary wall" isolating the city of Detroit. "I was surprised," she says, pausing. "And sad." So much of what leaders rely on—from their close community to their clear mission to their physical vitality—had been abruptly stripped away.

Lisa considers herself a Type A personality. She's willing to walk in obedience, even into dangerous or desolate places, but she needs a plan. "[God] is the author of creativity, and I look for that from Him," she says. In this season, it felt as though God had left her adrift.

She tried to persist in maintaining the relationships she had built and leading the Bible studies she had begun as a Youth for Christ staff member, wholeheartedly believing she could continue to minister with or without a paycheck. Yet "there were times when I just felt emotionally drained, like I had nothing to give," she recalls, identifying with Elijah and Moses, whose own wilderness seasons are well-documented in the Old Testament.

She would sink onto the family room couch and talk openly with God . . . or yell . . . or cry. "God, what are You doing?" she'd plead. She continued to seek, trusting she would find, and she continued to obey even when she didn't understand.

If vs. Though

Lisa was only a child when Martin Luther King Jr. preached his sermon "But If Not" at Ebenezer Baptist Church in Atlanta on November 5, 1967. But her life aligns with this message. It's a call to release the conditionalities of our obedience. King's sermon is based on the words of Shadrach, Meshach, and Abednego—three Jewish boys among the first forced into exile after Babylon conquered Jerusalem.

The Babylonian king, Nebuchadnezzar, obsessed with his power and ego, built a massive statue and demanded that everyone under his reign bow down when the music played. This is the same King Nebuchadnez-

> "The 'though' faith says, 'Though things go wrong; though evil is temporarily triumphant; though sickness comes and the cross looms, nevertheless! I'm gonna believe anyway and I'm gonna have faith anyway.'"

zar Jeremiah writes about, who destroyed Jerusalem in 586 BC. Knowing the wrath of this king, all obeyed the egomaniac's demand—except three young men.

Shadrach, Meshach, and Abednego responded, "If we are thrown into the blazing furnace, the God whom we serve is able to save us. He will rescue us from your power, Your Majesty. But even if he doesn't, we want to make it clear to you, Your Majesty, that we will never serve your gods or worship the gold statue you have set up."[5]

King's sermon focused on the difference between an "if" faith, which is full of conditionalities, and a "though" faith, modeled by these three men. King shared, "The 'if' faith says, 'If all goes well; if life is hopeful, prosperous and happy; if I don't have to go to jail; if I don't have to face the agonies and burdens of life; if I'm not ever called bad names because of taking a stand that I feel that I must take; if none of these things happen, then I'll have faith in God, then I'll be alright.'"[6]

This is not obedience. It is bargaining. Negotiating.

The alternative is a "though" faith. "The 'though' faith says, 'Though things go wrong; though evil is temporarily triumphant; though sickness comes and the cross looms, nevertheless! I'm gonna believe anyway and I'm gonna have faith anyway.'"[7]

King lived a life of faith and committed to obedience, regardless of the cost or consequences. This is the faith that sustained Lisa as well. Obey, regardless of the outcome.

Arguments with God

With the gift of hindsight, what felt like wilderness wandering is now something Lisa sees as a crucial time of preparation for what was to come. "God had to get so much out of me," she says. Slowly and painfully, she shed ego and identity wrapped up in her former leadership role and grew in her capacity to forgive and let go: all vital skills for what would come. "I was finally a vessel He could use," she says.

After years of uncertainty, Lisa was more than ready for a calling. But she didn't want the one she received. When God asked her to found a community development corporation, Lisa said no. God again told her yes. "And you never win an argument with God," she laughs.

"The journey of following Christ requires we dethrone me and enthrone Christ," shares Dr. Florence Muindi, founder of Life in Abundance International. "Our calling is not about our dreams and ambitions, but about seeking the Lord and listening to him in obedience."[8]

Lisa co-founded CDC in 1993 and describes the season that followed as "an incredible testimony to God's faithfulness and His love." Within the first year, Lisa had a front-row seat to God's miraculous provision for this ministry He had graciously entrusted to her. Volunteers pursued *them*, $100,000 in seed capital flowed in unsolicited, and children flocked to their ministry.

"Listen to my voice," God implored His people through Jeremiah, "and do all that I command you."[9]

In the almost three decades since its founding, Lisa listened and obeyed, and this has given her the opportunity to care for those in

172

poverty, feed the hungry, address health care disparities, and work toward more just race relations—responsibilities the Church has been slow to embrace. As Lisa and her team live out the biblical values outlined in Micah 6:8—to do justice, love mercy, and walk humbly with God—neighbors see something different in them. "You're seeing an impact on Edison Street . . . on Philadelphia Street . . . on Taylor Street . . . on Hazelwood Street, because we're all there," she says. Bit by bit, they're infusing the city with God's love.

"Sometimes I say I don't do anything else because there are no other options. This is it. God never said it was going to be beautiful and sweet and happily ever after," Lisa shares.

After twenty-six years as CDC's director, she is planning for her own succession. The 17 businesses established, 450 properties and homes rehabbed and repaired, and thousands of lives touched in central Detroit under her leadership are a testimony to her obedience and God's faithfulness. Even if it hasn't always been sweet, it has been good.

The Joy of Surrender

Lisa didn't understand what God was doing, especially in seasons of physical suffering, unclear direction, and hurt. She didn't understand God's ways or timing.

Yet she knew God was the potter and she the clay. She listened and obeyed even when she didn't understand. She lived a "though" faith, not an "if" faith.

Like Lisa, Jeremiah had seasons where he, too, couldn't understand God's plan. In the midst of lifelong persecution, mockery, and ridicule, Jeremiah obeyed even though he didn't understand.

The prophet is strikingly honest about the pain that accompanies his calling, yet he continues to look upward to God and press onward in obedience.

> O LORD, if you heal me, I will be truly healed;
>   if you save me, I will be truly saved.
>   My praises are for you alone!

> People scoff at me and say,
> "What is this 'message from the LORD' you talk about?
> 	Why don't your predictions come true?"
> LORD, I have not abandoned my job
> 	as a shepherd for your people.[10]

Jeremiah didn't see what God was doing and complained about how difficult his calling was, yet he obeyed. He couldn't avoid speaking the words God had given him. "[God's] word," Jeremiah writes, "burns in my heart like a fire. It's like a fire in my bones!"[11]

In our self-confident culture, we prize autonomy and independence. We celebrate initiative and drive. But obedience? Obedience isn't warmly embraced. Does God's Word burn in our very hearts and bones, driving us to action?

"Reared on a diet of rights and entitlements, we unwittingly expect God to cater to our needs," writes Alec Hill, president emeritus at InterVarsity USA. "But God owes us nothing. We owe him everything."[12]

What if obedience was actually a gift to us? We all serve something or someone; why not bow before our Maker and Redeemer instead of idols made by lesser kings?

There's no way that Jeremiah fully understood God's plan—yet he obeyed. He chose to kneel. To bow. To submit. To recognize that God is the ultimate authority, and we are not. "I know, LORD, that our lives are not our own. We are not able to plan our own course," Jeremiah confesses.[13]

Jeremiah looked up to "the only true God . . . the living God and the everlasting King,"[14] who stood "beside [him] like a great warrior."[15] In God's strength, Jeremiah pressed onward in obedience.

God invites us to do the same, trusting and obeying even when we don't understand. Even when we don't see exactly what God is doing.

Jeremiah's gritty obedience is built on trust in God and extends beyond difficult circumstances. That's the type of obedience Lisa discovered. She was following the words of an old-time gospel song, "I'm gonna do what the Spirit says do."[16]

Attentive Listening

Lisa developed an ability to listen attentively and patiently to God's prompting and leading. She made time and space, even in the challenges and disappointments, to seek God's guidance and direction. Her ears were open, and she was willing to listen to the answer.

Listening and then obeying is what Judah and Israel, and perhaps we, too, are so often unable to do. Even though God had sent Jeremiah to speak words of truth and perspective, the Israelites closed their ears.

God asks rhetorically, "Who will listen when I speak?" before adding, "Their ears are closed, and they cannot hear."[17]

The words conjure images of people who plugged their ears. Confident in their own capacity, they didn't think they wanted or needed God's direction and voice. Satisfied by their own strength, wisdom, and perspective, they closed their ears to God's call.

Despite God speaking to them, "again and again" they did not listen.[18] The result? They forgot their mission and identity—and were rendered useless.[19]

They failed to listen and failed to obey.

What caused Judah to shut their ears? What causes us to shut ours?

Ultimately, it's the illusion of our self-sufficiency. Our pride in our own intelligence and capacity. The idolizing of our own plans and perspectives. As the imagery of Jeremiah 17 reminds us, relying on human strength alone makes us like "stunted shrubs in the desert, with no hope for the future." An inward focus means we don't listen to God or to the people we serve.

For Judah and for us, Lisa and Jeremiah invite us to stop and listen. To realize that we are rendered useless on our own. For Lisa, there are open ears and open hands. She trusts her Father enough to hold her even when life doesn't make sense. She gets to work, delivering cookies and a desperately needed dose of hope as she presses on in obedience.

Application Questions

1. Do you have an "if" faith or a "though" faith? Why?

2. We all serve something or someone. Who do you feel you are being obedient to in this season of your life?

3. What fruit have you seen come from your obedience to God in the past?

4. What would it look like for you to regularly "attentively listen" to the voice of God?

5. Where in your life is God asking you to be obedient?

6. As you look to the future, what challenges might you face while seeking to obey God?

CHAPTER 18
PERSEVERANCE

At the timberline where the storms strike with the most fury, the sturdiest trees are found.

—Hudson Taylor[1]

In the years following World War II, the Philippines boasted one of the largest economies in Asia. While the rest of the continent reeled from the devastation of war, the Philippine economy thrived from growing industrial and agricultural production.

In the mid-1960s, Ferdinand Marcos, a rising political figure celebrated as a wartime hero, was elected president. He promised the Filipinos that the nation could "be great again," ending inequality and promoting an even faster-growing economy.[2]

Just a few years into his presidency, however, the economy began to crumble. The Marcos administration spent extravagantly, relying heavily on foreign loans. The gap between the Philippines' wealthiest and poorest citizens widened. As the country's economic state deteriorated, social unrest increased.

In response, Marcos declared martial law in 1972, promising to "build a new society."[3] Martial law gave him unlimited authority to make and enforce laws with the aid of the military. Portraying himself as a defender against communism, separatism, and disorder, Marcos initially garnered broad support.[4]

Over the next decade, he used the military to force citizens into submission. He arrested and jailed political opponents, looted billions of dollars from the economy—much of which remains unaccounted for—and imposed governmental control and ownership over all sectors of the Filipino economy. Marcos's reign devastated his country. Marcos wrote his own law, enacting hostile takeovers of major media, energy, food, and shipping companies.[5]

During Marcos's reign, "an estimated 34,000 trade unionists, student leaders, writers and politicians were tortured with electric shocks, heated irons and rape; 3,240 men and women were dumped dead in public places; 398 others simply disappeared," wrote investigative journalist Nick Davies in *The Guardian*.[6]

Some of Marcos's most embittered opponents were idealistic students incensed by his political corruption and his tightening chokehold on their liberties. As a student, Melba Maggay joined the student activist movement to resist the erosion of freedoms.

Communists and Dictators

Melba, who had come to faith while in college, dreamed of a Church that served the Kingdom first and foremost. "It's important to teach your people who they are and to whom they belong," Melba shares, "so they don't get lost. It's important not to lose that identity."

After Vietnam and Cambodia fell to communism in the 1960s, fear arose among Filipino Christians that their country would go the same way, limiting their freedom to worship. An evangelical leader spoke at Melba's church, urging congregants to praise and thank God for the country's martial law, since Marcos's regime protected their freedom to worship. The threat of communism had been held at bay. But in avoiding one broken system, they were asked to embrace another.

To Melba, many in the Church seemed apathetic toward, even complicit in, acts of injustice and political misuse of power. To Melba, injustices inflicted by communism *and* the Marcos dictatorship deserved protest. Disillusionment with the Church became a fog around her faith.

As she visited friends, fellow activists, and colleagues in prison, Melba's disillusionment continued to grow. She began working for a major newspaper, where her editor was one of those jailed for refusing to comply with new media restrictions. Other high-profile newspapers were also targeted for highlighting Marcos's abuse of power. In Melba's opinion, this was the role and responsibility not only of journalists but also of the Church.

She longed for the Church to defend the plight of the weak and vulnerable under this brutal dictatorship. But she did not allow disillusionment to grow into cynicism. Instead, she got to work, gathering a community of people who would consider the implications of the gospel in their cultural context. A small group of writers, theologians, social scientists, and other critical thinkers began the Institute for Studies in Asian Church and Culture (ISACC). The team of friends published a magazine, *Patmos*, which spurred fellow Christians to think biblically about justice and cultural issues.

"We needed fresh theological thinking rooted in our context and rooted in our faith," she shares. "We asked ourselves what it meant for the Kingdom of God to be present. How would it change our context?"

The response to their magazine surprised them.

"People called our publication evil. They accused us of being Marxists," Melba recounts. They failed to see that Melba wasn't advocating one form of flawed government over another. She was advocating for people of faith to stand up for those unfairly targeted and persecuted by an unjust regime. To Melba and ISACC, God's heart for justice transcended political ideologies.

Despite the opposition, the group remained unified in their mission. They continued to meet together, debate current issues, and publish their learnings. Reactions only worsened.

After months of working together under harsh criticism, many gave up. Six months in, Melba was ready to call it quits, too.

But around that time, she received two letters offering a new perspective and helping her clarify her course. In the first, a missionary working among a Filipino tribe in the Cordillera mountains shared that he had read the cohort's work and been encouraged to continue in his ministry. The group's thinking about contextualizing the gospel aligned with some of his own and gave voice to things he hadn't been able to articulate. "It's good to have a community thinking about this," the letter concluded.

Another letter came from a pastor working in a Muslim-majority community in the southern part of the country. He admitted he'd been feeling very lonely as he grappled with justice issues in his context. The letter—though sent from a different person and place—concluded like the first: "I'm glad to learn there's a group of people doing something about this."

God used those letters to reanimate Melba's passion, helping her persevere. She heard the Lord speak to her, "If only for those people, you must continue."

Though she found her hope renewed, the challenges she faced did not evaporate. The members continued to be accused of being Marxists, and as a result, many people refused to support the ministry.

Some criticized them because ISACC was led by a woman; others criticized the organization for its exclusively Filipino leadership team. Some questioned its ability to last without foreign funding.

Yet God called Melba to persevere. The remaining team stubbornly clung to their vision and the assurance that their work mattered. After years of slogging through false accusations and public rebuke, they would soon have the chance to put their theories into practice.

Buying Land amid a Siege

Nobody called Jeremiah a Marxist, but much like Melba, everyone ridiculed him. Jeremiah writes that he became a "household joke" and was "mocked every day."[7] A priest named Pashur put Jeremiah in stocks at the Benjamin Gate to facilitate public shaming.[8]

Jeremiah does not hold back in questioning why God could allow him to experience such pain.

Why then does my suffering continue?
　　Why is my wound so incurable?
Your help seems as uncertain as a seasonal brook,
　　like a spring that has gone dry.[9]

"We don't have to like it. Jeremiah didn't like it," writes Eugene Peterson. "He yelled at Pashur [the priest], and after he yelled at Pashur he yelled at God, angry, hurt and somewhat bewildered that all this was happening to him. He didn't like any of it, but he wasn't afraid of it because the most important thing in his life was God—not comfort, not applause, not security, but the living God. What he did fear was . . . missing what God wanted. It is still the only thing worthy of our fear."[10]

Late in his life, Jeremiah was once again locked in chains as the Babylonian army besieged Jerusalem.[11] In a terrible situation only getting worse, God gives Jeremiah hope.

God instructs Jeremiah to do the unthinkable: purchase property. Again, Jeremiah questions God.[12] He looked at his circumstances and saw that the Babylonians controlled Jerusalem and this field at Anathoth.[13]

Still, Jeremiah purchases the land for seventeen shekels of silver, which, considering the circumstances, we hope was a steeply discounted price. Jeremiah buys this plot of land, even though it is occupied by Israel's enemies.

God instructs Jeremiah, "Take these documents, both the sealed and unsealed copies of the deed of purchase, and put them in a clay jar so they will last a long time."[14]

The directive only makes sense if God's people were to one day inhabit this land again. It was a sign of hope.

"For this is what the LORD Almighty, the God of Israel, says: Houses, fields and vineyards will again be bought in this land."[15]

You don't purchase land when you're under siege and preparing to leave your homeland. But God promised an eventual return. Even more significant, God promised restoration, forgiveness, and grace. Beyond healing the land, God would bring healing to their hearts, too. "I will cleanse them from all the sin they have committed against me and will forgive all their sins of rebellion against me. Then this city will bring me renown, joy, praise and honor before all nations on earth that hear of all the good things I do for it."[16]

Inhabitants of Jerusalem most certainly felt overwhelmed by pain and hurt as they were forced into captivity. They wept at the loss of their homeland, the destruction of the Temple—the visible dwelling place of their God. Likely they had abandoned hope. Many gave up on their nation and on their God and His promises to them.

But Jeremiah pointed them to an eventual return to their land and to forgiveness. And lastly, Jeremiah points to a "righteous descendant,"[17] who one day would provide ultimate healing and restoration. If this physical return and restoration were not enough reason to hold on to hope, Jeremiah points to an even more significant future blessing, not in a return of their land but in a Savior.

Amid ridicule and setbacks, God gave Jeremiah glimpses of hope for future restoration of the land and the promise of a coming Savior. And God was about to give Melba and ISACC similar glimpses of hope in their community.

People Power Revolution

After twenty years of corrupt leadership under Ferdinand Marcos—including almost a decade and a half of martial law—Filipinos had had enough. For four days in February 1986, over a million Filipinos took to the streets, seeking to overthrow the corrupt regime.

The movement, called the People Power Revolution, followed the assassination of Benigno (Ninoy) Aquino, an outspoken critic of Marcos. When Aquino's widow, Corazon C. Aquino, ran against Marcos in an election in early 1986, she gained a massive following. Marcos declared himself the winner amid charges of electoral fraud. Protests cropped up nationwide.

Steadfast in their convictions, Melba and the ISACC community remained consistent in criticizing the abuse and injustice around them. They joined the mounting protests in the streets. Some fellow evangelical leaders criticized ISACC for their "rebellion," yet the team remained active in writing and in protesting. After four days of peaceful protests, justice prevailed in the Philippines. Marcos fled the country, and the process of rebuilding finally began.

Following the People Power Revolution, the tide started to turn for ISACC. While continuing to conduct research and draft publications on their understanding of biblical justice, they also offered courses and training in political advocacy and community transformation. As their work became more well known, funds began pouring in from places as far away as Germany and the Netherlands.

Since their founding, ISACC has trained hundreds of practitioners, churches, and faith-based organizations in community and economic development. They have consistently promoted faith in action, emphasizing the Great Commission and the Great Commandment.

They've had plenty of opportunities to put their beliefs into action, especially as they serve alongside local communities after natural disasters. In 1990, when an earthquake wiped out thousands of acres of crops and piled tons of debris onto the roads, ISACC worked with the indigenous communities to rebuild and restore. With ISACC's assistance, the local tribes cleared the roads, revitalized their farms, and started four multi-purpose cooperatives. When Typhoon Haiyan struck in 2013—killing over 6,000 Filipinos and leaving close to $3 billion of damage in its wake—ISACC immediately sent teams to engage in rehabilitation and trauma care in Tacloban, one of the most devastated communities.

ISACC also continues to build capacity among the urban poor communities. When Batasan, the third largest slum community in the Philippines, was plagued by fifty street gangs, ISACC intervened to offer psychological support and biblical teaching. Gang wars, crime, drug use, and petty theft dropped in the area, and transformed youth in the community organized to foster a culture of peace and even began a church that continues to thrive. ISACC has also launched microenterprise programs to support hundreds of vulnerable families in a remote fishing community.[18]

Eugene Peterson writes about this type of long-term faithful service.

> Jeremiah did not resolve to stick it out for twenty-three years, no matter what. He got up every morning with the sun. The day was God's day, not

the people's. He didn't get up to face rejection; he got up to meet with God. He didn't rise to put up with another round of mockery, he rose to be with his Lord. That is the secret of his persevering pilgrimage—not thinking with dread about the long road ahead but greeting the present moment, every present moment, with obedient delight, with expectant hope: "My heart is ready!"[19]

In her own persevering pilgrimage, Melba credits not only the importance of regular rhythms of worship and prayer but also faith integration in her work. "Our faith must impact the day-to-day processes, operations, and management," she says.

Melba's desire is for the community to see ISACC first and foremost as followers of Jesus in the work they do—to see their fruit as the result of their connection to the good soil and the Living Water. With clarity and conviction, they are pursuing their mission to "creatively witness to the Lordship of Jesus in all of life by penetrating cultures with the values of the Kingdom and engaging the powers towards social transformation."[20]

Our Hope Springs Eternal

Melba testifies to the friends who have walked with her through the most challenging seasons, the spiritual mentors who reminded her that Christianity isn't the four walls of a church, and the books that opened her eyes to a larger vision of Christian mission.

And then she pointed to another, more powerful force: love. "When I was younger, I was more certain about many things, but as I get older, I've realized there are fewer and fewer things I can really be certain about. But there's one thing I've become more convinced of the older I grow: The Lord loves me in a very personal way. Whatever challenge, whatever frustration, the Lord loves me—and this sustains me."

In reflecting on her forty-two years with ISACC, she rests in knowing God called her to this work.

"We may suffer setbacks. We may suffer defeat. These are the kinds of things Satan inflicts on us because he is on the retreat; he's finished.

Revelation tells us that, though we may lose some battles, we will win the war. That gives me hope."

Unlike Melba, Jeremiah never saw the fulfilment of his hopes in his community. It would be over a century after Jeremiah's death when Ne-

> "There's one thing I've become more convinced of the older I grow: The Lord loves me in a very personal way."

hemiah and a faithful remnant of God's people would rebuild the Holy City of Jerusalem and consecrate the Temple and city to God. It would be five centuries until the "righteous descendant" arrived in Bethlehem.

> "For the time is coming,"
>   says the LORD,
> "when I will raise up a righteous descendant
>   from King David's line.
> He will be a King who rules with wisdom.
>   He will do what is just and right throughout the land.
> And this will be his name:
>   'The LORD Is Our Righteousness.'
> In that day Judah will be saved,
>   and Israel will live in safety."[21]

This King arrived to usher in His reign of wisdom, justice, and protection. Like Jeremiah, we also wait for the full and final consummation of Jesus' reign. And while we wait, we buy land, defend the vulnerable, and look upward to the sustaining love of God.

Today, Melba and the ISACC community continue to persevere to see the hope of the gospel bring social transformation across Asia. "We still have much work to do," Melba says, "but this is what it means for us to stand for the Kingdom in our time."

Application Questions

1. Where have you seen perseverance, or a lack of perseverance, impact your community, country, or culture?
2. Who do you know who maintains strong perseverance? What can you learn from these individuals?
3. When you attempt to persevere, what are you hoping to attain and where do you look for strength?
4. What fruit have you seen in your life from perseverance in the past?
5. In what areas of your life do you need to pray for greater perseverance? Why?

CHAPTER 19
COMMUNITY

Christian community is the place where we keep the flame of hope alive among us and take it seriously so that it can grow and become stronger in us.

—Henri Nouwen[1]

was confused about life. I was violent, a hooligan," shares Marek Kucharski. "I became so unhappy that I decided to kill myself. The last thing I planned to do was come back home and say goodbye to my twin brother."

Marek grew up in a small town in northwest Poland during communist times. To his knowledge, there were no Christians in his community, and hope was in almost equally short supply. As teenagers, Marek and his friends abused alcohol, and many of their peers found an escape through drugs. Violence plagued their community. At age eighteen, Marek grew so weary with his life that he decided to end it. When he returned home to say goodbye to his twin brother, however, his brother shared something that altered Marek's trajectory entirely.

"My brother approached me before I could share my plans with him and said, 'Marek, there's someone who loves you.'"

His brother would go on to share the good news with Marek, introducing him to Jesus Christ, the One who loved Marek before Marek even knew of Him. The concept of salvation by grace was unheard of in his community, and this hope of the gospel astonished Marek—and saved his life. Not everything changed that day. But over the ensuing years, Marek began to understand Christ's love for him. And his life began to change dramatically. In the years that followed, Marek shared this good news with his friends and community.

Many joined Marek in exchanging a life of hopelessness for a life of faithful obedience to their newfound Savior. For some, this meant walking away from drugs and violence. For others, it meant clinging to the truth of the gospel when their families believed something else entirely. For all who believed, this was a radical, countercultural change that they lived out daily. Each weekend, Marek and his friends would travel hours by train to attend church. Communism had just collapsed in Eastern Europe, and the hunger for meaning and purpose surged among Marek's neighbors.

Still, the spiritual climate in Poland remains largely dormant. For most people in Poland, faith remains more cultural than personal. Today, just 0.3% of Poles identify as evangelical Christian,[2] and according to a study by Pew Research Center, just 16% of young Catholics in Poland[3] say their faith is important to them.[4] And the forecast is even more dire. The percentage of people attending church or mass is dropping more rapidly in Poland than any other country in the world.[5]

Dr. Andrzej Turkanik, a native of Poland, serves as the director of Quo Vadis Institute, an Austrian nonprofit dedicated to helping Christian cultural influencers from a variety of professions find common ground to engage the most demanding challenges facing a fragmented Europe.

"Europe is an incredible continent," shares Turkanik. "Unfortunately, in the last 150 years in Europe, an ideology that says 'God is dead' has replaced much of the Christian story. . . . We end up today in a twilight zone, where Europe is the first post-Christian society in the world."[6]

Hope remains dim for Christian leaders throughout Europe. But for leaders like Marek and Turkanik, hope is kept alive in community.

An Expanded Vision for Poland

Several years after Marek began attending church, he felt God calling him to plant a church in his hometown. To prepare himself for that venture, he attended Evangelical School of Theology (EST), a school established by missionaries in Wrocław, Poland, and, after graduating, planted a church in this community where hopelessness once reigned. He served there for nine years.

Seeing how the gospel could transform entire communities, Marek sensed God's call to train and equip fellow Polish believers with the skills to take the hope of Jesus throughout Europe. To accomplish that mission and pursue that hope, he accepted an invitation to return to his seminary in the role of chancellor.

For the last fifteen years, Marek has served in senior leadership roles at the school. Located in one of Poland's largest cities, EST graduates dozens of Polish students into careers in pastoral ministry, Christian publishing, media, and the arts.

Building a seminary, recruiting and leading a team, and raising the funding to support the school has been deeply fulfilling to Marek as he's seen Christian leaders graduate into positions of influence in the deeply secular culture surrounding the school. But the journey has not been without challenges. For Marek, the most significant challenges along his leadership journey have occurred at home, not at work.

Hope at Work, Tragedy at Home

"I'll be frank," Marek shares. "The most difficult challenges came in my private life. In the beginning it was small, but with time, it became a family nightmare."

Marek and his wife have two sons. When their oldest son entered his teenage years, they began to see concerning trends in his behavior. He was rebellious and increasingly withdrawn. Eventually the situation reached a breaking point, and their seventeen-year-old son checked into a yearlong drug treatment center. Following a month of no contact (mandated as part of the treatment regimen), the family was permitted a visit and drove to the treatment center. While visiting, they learned—to their complete shock—that their younger son also struggled with a crippling drug addiction. Marek and his wife drove home alone.

"In one day, we lost two sons," Marek says. "When I returned home, I crashed, cried, and was absolutely broken."

The tragedy at home challenged everything Marek believed. It challenged everything he taught.

"I would take my sons to school when they were young boys and pray for them not to take drugs," Marek says. "Then, that kind of thing hits you even when you are doing your duty for God's Kingdom. That's a conflict. Your system of faith and everything gets challenged. I was praying. Where did that prayer go? Did it get lost?"

Marek and his wife describe this season as the darkest in their lives. There were tears nearly every day for months as they prayed and hoped and longed for their sons to overcome addiction.

The temptation leaders often face when dealing with personal crises is to lean harder into their work and to attempt, through gritted teeth,

> The gift of community can reorient us, guiding us onward when our vision is clouded, when our view is obscured, or even when we aren't sure we have the strength to look up.

to overcome these challenges alone. But as mentor and coach Dave Jewitt notes, isolation is "prime picking for the enemy."[7]

Marek pursued the opposite path. When facing this tragedy at home, Marek permitted himself a pace of greater balance and rest from work and chose to lean more fully into his community. "We need your support," Marek would share honestly with trusted friends and colleagues.

"I've been a leader. I've even been leading you. But now I'm asking for you to call me every once in a while and ask how I feel."

The ensuing months were challenging for Marek and his family. They sustained and nurtured their faith through prayer and in community, inviting support where they felt weak. They pressed onward, surrounded by believers who helped them sense Christ's closeness even in the valley. The Kucharscys understood the chances their sons would beat their addictions were quite low. And, while they hoped for the best, they knew there were no guarantees God would answer their prayers in the way they desired. But against the statistical odds for recovery, both of their sons persevered through treatment. They've now been clean for more than six years.

"I believe hope is like this: We are drifting on a boat, and hope is something constant like the land far away," Marek shares. "We know it is there, even if we have not gotten there yet. Sometimes things get challenging on the boat; there are big waves, and you lose sight of the land. But the land is still there."

The gift of community can reorient us, guiding us onward when our vision is clouded, when our view is obscured, or even when we aren't sure we have the strength to look up.

Hope for Europe

At Evangelical School of Theology, the work of training leaders in the faith continues. The school was co-founded by missionaries to Poland. And for many years the faculty was composed of expatriate missionaries teaching at the school. Today, however, the staff is almost entirely Polish leaders teaching students from their own country.

Between sixty and eighty students enroll at the seminary each year. At seminary, they confront existential questions about their faith— and the ensuing questions arising from Europe's increasingly secular culture.

"There is hope," shares Turkanik. "With secularization taking place in Europe, there is also a new movement where churches have been planted in some of the most secularized places. We have refugees coming to faith and creating new communities of faith."[8]

Leaders like Marek and Turkanik inhabit a place where hope often feels distant. It feels like that distant land across a tumultuous ocean. While they know it's there, seeing it can sometimes be difficult.

"Even though I don't see the land today because I'm going through shaky times, the land still exists," says Marek. "It's only because the wave is too big and it covers my view. But I have the promise from Jesus that the land is there."

Community of Hope

Jeremiah was given an exceptionally unpopular task: speak God's truth to a nation that simply didn't want to hear it. Undoubtedly, there were moments of isolation as he faithfully followed this call. "He is, for the most part, the only prophet of God in the land: everyone else who claims to have a word from the Lord is a fake," writes biblical commentator Jeffrey Kranz. "That's especially difficult for Jeremiah, because while the false prophets preach peace, safety, and victory over Babylon, Jeremiah insists that the Babylonians will destroy everything. The false prophets tell everyone that God is with His people; Jeremiah tells everyone that God is on the enemy's side. You can imagine which message is more popular."[9]

For the hard truths he delivered, Jeremiah was largely despised and isolated. "Violent words and acts against the prophet come from within his home community, Anathoth," writes Samuel Hildebrandt, "from the religious officials and from those in political power."[10]

But in chapter 32, we meet Baruch: a faithful friend, companion, and supporter. Baruch even played a role in transcribing Jeremiah's prophecies.[11] When Jeremiah was banned by King Jehoiakim from preaching, it was Baruch who showed up and took his place.[12] When Jeremiah was told to go into hiding, Baruch went with him.[13] Even when going into exile, the two went together.[14]

Baruch and Jeremiah persevered together. And not just the two of them, but there are glimpses of other friends as well. An influential man named Ahikam saves Jeremiah from the wrath of the authorities.[15] When Jeremiah is stuck in the mud (literally) at the bottom of a cistern, it is a servant named Ebed-Melech who helps provide rescue by pleading Jeremiah's case to the king. Ebed-Melech was from the land of Cush, modern-day Ethiopia, and was a cross-cultural friend who showed up in Jeremiah's moment of greatest need.[16] Although he was a foreigner and in the service of King Zedekiah, his greater allegiance was to a different King.

Jeremiah was promised God's presence at the beginning of his work, and he is also given the gift of friendships along the way.

As we spoke to global leaders who had persevered amid prevalent trials and setbacks, they were quick to share that they did not go it alone. In fact, they often pushed back when we asked them to tell us *their* story. It was evident that each leader was buoyed by a community that nurtured hope. The stories are never just of individuals but always have a collective component. It's not just about resilient and hopeful people; it's about resilient and hopeful communities. It's about meeting needs in the world and meeting needs in each other.

Jeremy Courtney, founder and CEO of Preemptive Love, has witnessed almost unspeakable atrocities in nations fractured by war.

"How do you sustain hope in this work that you're doing?" queried an interviewer.

"That's actually pretty easy," Courtney replied. And then he spoke of community. "I'm never in it alone. It's never me in my head, left to my own devices to decide, *Am I going to hope or not? . . .* There's always a different voice that can speak up at a different time and say, '*Let's keep going forward.*' It's together in action that the hope is sustained."[17]

Friendship is sacred. God did not design us to walk alone. Enduring hope involves growing together. Individualism will eventually let us down; if we are going to last, we need a collective resilience and a community of hope.

Loneliness is on the rise—with deadly consequences. Some researchers have reported that loneliness and social isolation can be as damaging to health as smoking fifteen cigarettes a day.[18] It's twice as dangerous as obesity. Isolation impairs immune functions, boosts inflammation, and has been linked to arthritis, type 2 diabetes, and heart disease. There are health consequences of trying to do life alone.

Isolation creeps steadily forward—and social media shouting matches do little but reinforce echo chambers of loneliness, cynicism, and disillusionment. In this moment, we find ourselves longing for something more. Isolationism and individualism are deeply disappointing, leaving us thirsty for lasting relationships.

"Suffering is upon all of us," shares Dr. Michael Badriaki, founder of The Global Leadership Community.[19] "We need to pray together, to eat together, to cry together, to mourn together as much as possible. We will bury our loved ones together. That's how the story changes."

In Jeremiah and in our interviews, we heard about a beautiful belonging. About giving yourself to not just a cause but a community.

When you experience drought conditions, you know who your true friends are. As Proverbs 17:17 relates, "Friends love through all kinds of weather, and families stick together in all kinds of trouble" (MSG). Or as the Burundian proverb summarizes, "You'll never make it through the dry season on your own."

Over time, we become like the community we are part of. So we choose those relationships with discernment, and we remember that the ultimate relationship is the one with our Creator.

Leaders who last in the midst of drought conditions accept God's good gift of doing life in community.

Application Questions

1. How have you seen community impact your life?
2. Do you actively lean into community on a regular basis? If not, what is holding you back?
3. Who are the people you turn to when you need help or want to celebrate something?

4. If you need more people to do life with, how can you gain a greater community? What churches, organizations, or events will you explore?

5. Who do you know who needs to be invited into your community?

CONCLUSION

Finding Hope

The bad news will not stop. But dire headlines don't tell the whole story. Around the world, followers of Christ continue to run toward suffering regardless of the cost. They continue to live and share the hope of the gospel—the good news—reminding us that God is showing up, bringing redemption and healing to our world. May we remember and retell these stories of enduring hope and, even more so, may we live them.

"Remember your leaders who taught you the word of God," wrote the author of Hebrews. "Think of all the good that has come from their lives, and follow the example of their faith."[1]

The stories we've shared are more than inspirational. They are directional: pointing us toward the God who sustains, inviting us to follow their examples of faith. "God's call is not designed to make us supermen and superwomen, because that's not what the world needs; it needs men and women who are humble enough, and often that means humbled enough . . . not to impose a solution on the world from a great height but to live within the world as it is, allowing the ambiguities and the perplexities of their own sense or absence of vocation to be nevertheless the place where they listen for the voice of God, and struggle to obey as best they can," writes N. T. Wright.[2]

We don't need more "superheroes" to respond to those in need, but we will need sustained strength—and we won't find it in our idealism, disillusionment, or cynicism. We need enduring hope, and it's in these times of acknowledging our own insufficiency in the face of great need that we are most likely to find it. Though painful, our difficult circumstances and limitations point us toward real and sustaining hopefulness—because they invite us to Jesus.

We don't long for more when we feel satiated. We don't fervently cry out to God when we operate within our own strength. Could this moment of thirst point us to the Living Water?

In Matthew 11:28–30, Jesus invites, "Are you tired? Worn out? Burned out on religion? Come to me. Get away with me and you'll recover your life. I'll show you how to take a real rest. Walk with me and work with me—watch how I do it. Learn the unforced rhythms of grace. I won't lay anything heavy or ill-fitting on you. Keep company with me and you'll learn to live freely and lightly."[3]

As we step into the significant work of loving others, we simply cannot do it by looking more deeply within ourselves. We cannot tighten our laces enough to run this race or survive this journey. Our only path forward is one empowered by the Spirit, rooted in Christ, and aligned with the unforced rhythms of grace.

God promises to use all things—including moments of great success and moments of gut-wrenching pain—for our good and His glory.[4] Let's turn upward and outward, pressing onward, knowing God is with us even when we ache and walk through dark valleys. As Madeleine L'Engle wrote, let us "live in such a way that [our] life would not make sense if God did not exist."[5]

We hope Christ's followers will, yes, run toward the suffering and hurting—but run first toward Christ, drawing from Him the strength to journey for decades, not days. We long to be people who invite our gracious Savior to refresh and nourish our weary souls as we respond to the needs around us. To live fearlessly and love boldly because we trust that God is with us. To press into the costly work of *loving like Jesus* precisely because we are *loved by Jesus*.

Rediscovering Foster Care

When my family hit our pain threshold with foster care, I (Peter) was ready to give up. Yet God's grace invaded our home once again, healing our wounds and drawing us through that season of disillusionment.

At our lowest moment, as I laid out my best arguments to God and my family on why foster care wasn't for us, my daughter Lili, at age eleven, spoke the words I needed to hear. "Dad, you're only looking at this from your perspective."

She was right. My fears and concerns focused on me: my family, my safety, my home, my future. Subconsciously, I had turned inward. I had lost sight of the kids and of the God who loves them infinitely more than I ever could.

Lili's reminder prompted me to look up. And as I did, God reminded me of His love and presence—even in our pain. With less directness than Jeremiah spoke to Judah, God confronted my preoccupation with safety and security. Like the Israelites, I had lost sight of the mission to care for others and instead given in to the fear of an uncertain future. My idealism did not sustain me, disillusionment caused me to question everything, and cynicism crept in.

Love always decenters our preoccupation with ourselves, providing an alternative center of gravity. As the apostle Paul writes, love "always protects, always trusts, always hopes, always perseveres."[6] This isn't about our ability to grit it out; in our own strength, we are unable to "always"—or even most of the time—protect, trust, hope, and persevere.

My family's invitation, like the one extended to the Israelites in Jeremiah, was to dislocate ourselves from the center of the story. To focus not on our strength, abilities, or grit, which cannot sustain us when intense difficulties come. And to recognize by God's grace that our inability to serve "in our own strength" is not a design flaw but an invitation to deepen our roots in Christ.

When we are at the center of our own stories, trying to serve in our own strength, we inevitably come up short. Self-absorption is toxic. It is what caused Judah to turn inward, prompting both God's rebuke as well as the grace-filled invitation: "Return to Me."

Then and now, the invitation is to walk away from our leaky cisterns and return to the Living Water. To let our service flow not from our abilities and resolve but from our rootedness in the Source of sustaining love.

If we're at the center, we love as long as others love us back. We will serve as long as we're recognized. We will give as long as we're properly thanked. There are conditions in our commitment. But these are transactions, not love.

Faithful leaders who last don't believe in conditionality. They do not attach strings. They discover a love devoid of forced reciprocity or fine print. In a rancorous world, this ability to love and serve with

> If we're at the center, we love as long as others love us back. We will serve as long as we're recognized. We will give as long as we're properly thanked. There are conditions in our commitment. But these are transactions, not love.

no expectations will turn heads and move hearts. When God is at the center, our ability to turn outward and respond with true compassion dramatically increases.

The invitation to Judah is the invitation to us today: "Return to Me." And then allow God's love to fill you with an enduring hope that spills over in sacrificial service.

Glimpses of Grace

We know there are absolutely no promises of happy endings on our timelines, but sometimes we do see glimpses of God's grace.

Shortly after our family reengaged in foster care, we met a seven-year-old named London. After two years in foster care, she needed a permanent home. She initially spent weekends at our home but officially moved in on December 20, 2019. A few days later, she opened her gifts on Christmas morning, and we celebrated as a new family. With the wrapping paper still littering the floor, I asked London what her favorite gift was, quite confident it was an epic dollhouse.

But her answer brought everything to a halt.

"I've never had a daddy before!" she responded.

That was the best gift either of us received that year.

When we disengage or give in to cynicism, we might protect ourselves from potential pain, but we also guarantee that we will miss the beautiful moments. The breakthroughs. The miracles. The healing. They're never promised, rarely expected, yet oftentimes are more meaningful than we could ever imagine. Had we given up in our most difficult season, we would have missed this moment and thousands of other moments, too.

Faithful service requires us to walk into pain. To feel the hurt. To see the reasons to despair. To know suffering, disappointment, and challenges. And yet to cling with desperation to the God of hope.

Ultimately, God alone can rescue the cynic and redirect the disillusioned.

In your journey, may you discover that "hope will not lead to disappointment. For we know how dearly God loves us, because he has given us the Holy Spirit to fill our hearts with his love."[7]

Turn upward and you will discover that there is always Hope.

ACKNOWLEDGMENTS

This endeavor, like the previous books we wrote together, is possible because of the amazing team surrounding us. While our names are on the spine, we unequivocally could not have done this without the support of our incredible team. We want to put the world's biggest asterisk alongside our names as authors of this book. Like the leaders we featured in the book, we wrote it from, with, and because of the community around us.

Jill Heisey and Brianna Lapp served as collaborators, advisors, writers, editors, counselors (!), cheerleaders, and coaches from the genesis of the idea. More than any project we've undertaken, this one saw the book's big ideas twist and turn over the course of our research. Jill and Brianna: Thank you for your patience, wisdom, and kindness throughout this harrowing journey! Your contributions to the book are innumerable, but it's the steadfastness of your character and *your* enduring hope in Christ and in this project that we most cherish.

Our amazing interns and fellows—Sarah Woodard, Sarah Beth Spraggins, and Adrian Schunk—each joined at critical junctures in the journey. Sarah did significant foundational research for this project back at its beginning. Sarah Beth helped us with early interviews and with the initial direction of the book. And Adrian carried the baton beautifully down the homestretch.

This is our third rodeo with our literary agent, Andrew Wolgemuth at Wolgemuth and Associates, and our editor, Andy McGuire, at Bethany House. We are so fortunate to have these two leaders in our corner. Their professionalism and skill in their craft are evident, but it was their words of encouragement at key junctures that we appreciated most. Thanks for believing in us and for believing in this project.

Our families endured our personal journey from idealism through disillusionment to enduring hope over the course of writing the book. We both had moments of frustration, confusion, and exhaustion while trying to put this book together. They helped us navigate our disillusionment and find hope even in the project itself. We are so thankful for Laurel, Keith, Lili, Myles, and London, and for Alli, Desmond, Abe, Juni, and Mack.

We each had foundational conversations early in the ideation process. Daniel Rice suggested we consider Jeremiah 17 as an anchor text. Dan Williams proposed we examine the ways disillusionment may be a gift. Many other friends and colleagues helped to strengthen our thinking and clarify our perspective.

On our own, we could not have met the amazing leaders we interviewed for this book. Our sincere thanks to Chad Hayward, Katelyn Beaty, Harlan VanOort, Chilobe Kalambo, Durwood Snead, Francis Kaitano, Lisa Espineli Chinn, Tim Hoiland, Rob Gailey, Tyler Green, Hunter Beaumont, Candy Sparks, and Lesly Jules for each opening their networks to us.

We're grateful to the team of readers whose early edits, questions, and critiques made the book what it is. In particular, we're grateful for Claire Stewart, Phil Smith, Ashley Dickens, Pat Ryan, and Mark Cunningham. Thanks to Benj Petroelje for introducing us to Dr. Samuel Hildebrandt, a scholar and theologian whose invaluable understanding of and passion for Jeremiah helped to make sure we got Jeremiah right.

Our talented colleague Jeff Brown helped bring order from the chaos. His design of the journey illustrations used throughout the book enabled its big ideas to finally arrange themselves. While the Froot Loops metaphor did not make it into the book itself, it lives forever in these acknowledgments.

Finally, our thanks to our amazing interviewees: Florence Muindi, Bill Massaquoi, Dickens Thunde, Eris Labady, Michael Badriaki, Jo Anne Lyon, Farai Mutamiri, Camille Melki, Melba Maggay, Phil Thuma, Tita Evertsz, Chris Brewster, Marek Kucharski, Tass Saada, Lisa Johanon, Edouard Lassegue, Ann Saylor, and Riaan. You point us to the God of hope.

ABOUT THE AUTHORS

Peter Greer is the president and CEO of HOPE International, a global Christ-centered economic development organization serving throughout Africa, Asia, Latin America, and Eastern Europe.

Prior to joining HOPE, Peter worked internationally as a microfinance adviser in Cambodia and Zimbabwe and as managing director for Urwego Bank in Rwanda. He received a BS in international business from Messiah University and an MPP in political and economic development from Harvard's Kennedy School.

Peter's favorite part of his job is spending time with the entrepreneurs HOPE serves—whether harvesting coffee with farmers in Rwanda, dancing alongside savings groups in Haiti, or visiting the greenhouses of entrepreneurs in Ukraine.

As an advocate for the Church's role in missions and alleviating extreme poverty, Peter has coauthored fourteen books, including *Mission Drift* (selected as a 2015 Book Award Winner from *Christianity Today*), *Rooting for Rivals* (selected as a 2019 Leadership Resource of the Year in *Outreach* magazine), *The Spiritual Danger of Doing Good* (selected as one of the Top 40 books on poverty by *World* magazine), and *Created to Flourish* (which his mom reviewed with five stars and a smiley face emoji).

More important than his role at HOPE is his role as husband to Laurel and dad to Keith, Liliana, Myles, and London. While his sports loyalties remain in New England, Peter and his family live in Lancaster, PA.

Learn more at peterkgreer.com, on Twitter (@peterkgreer), and on Facebook (facebook.com/peterkgreer).

Chris Horst is the chief advancement officer at HOPE International, where he employs his passion for advancing initiatives at the intersection of faith and work. In addition to his role at HOPE, Chris spends an alarming percentage of his free time tending to his yard with all the loving care normally afforded to newborn children. He and his wife, Alli, have four human children of whom they are even prouder than their lawn—Desmond, Abe, Juni, and Mack. As a dad to four kiddos, Chris has recently undergone a radical transformation from self-proclaimed foodie to a man who prepares far more trays of chicken nuggets than avocado toast. He wouldn't change it.

Chris serves on the board of the Mile High WorkShop; has been published in *The Denver Post* and *Christianity Today*; and has coauthored the books *Mission Drift, Entrepreneurship for Human Flourishing,* and *Rooting for Rivals* with Peter Greer. *Christianity Today, World* magazine, and the Evangelical Christian Publishers Association named *Mission Drift* a Book of the Year in 2015. Chris was a very average student, but he did graduate with both a bachelor's degree from Taylor University and an MBA from Bakke Graduate University.

ABOUT HOPE INTERNATIONAL

HOPE International invests in the dreams of families in the world's underserved communities as we proclaim and live the gospel. We provide discipleship, biblically based training, savings services, and small loans, empowering women and men to use the skills God has placed in their hands to provide for their families and strengthen their communities.

Proceeds from this book support HOPE International. For more information, please visit hopeinternational.org.

RECOMMENDED RESOURCES FOR FURTHER STUDY

Bringle, Mary L. *Despair: Sickness or Sin? Hopelessness and Healing in the Christian Life*. Nashville, TN: Abingdon Press, 1990.

Brooks, David. *The Second Mountain: The Quest for a Moral Life*. New York, NY: Random House, 2019.

Brueggemann, Walter. *Hopeful Imagination: Prophetic Voices in Exile*. Philadelphia, PA: Fortress Press, 1986.

———. *Like Fire in the Bones: Listening to the Prophetic Word in Jeremiah*. Minneapolis, MN: Fortress Press, 2011.

Duckworth, Angela. *Grit: The Power of Passion and Perseverance*. New York, NY: Scribner Book Company, 2016.

Hanson, Rick. *Resilient: How to Grow an Unshakable Core of Calm, Strength, and Happiness*. New York, NY: Harmony, 2018.

Idleman, Kyle. *Don't Give Up: Faith That Gives You the Confidence to Keep Believing and the Courage to Keep Going*. Grand Rapids, MI: Baker Books, 2019.

Kaiser Jr., Walter C. *Walking in the Ancient Paths: A Commentary on Jeremiah*. Bellingham, WA: Lexham Press, 2019.

Kidner, Derek. *The Message of Jeremiah*. The Bible Speaks Today. Downers Grove, IL: InterVarsity Press, 1987.

Lynch, William F. *Images of Hope: Imagination as Healer of the Hopeless*. Montreal: Palm Publishers, 1965.

MacDonald, Gordon. *A Resilient Life: You Can Move Forward No Matter What*. Nashville, TN: Thomas Nelson, 2009.

McConville, J. Gordon. *Judgment and Promise: An Interpretation of the Book of Jeremiah*. Leicester, England: Apollos, 1993.

O'Connor, Kathleen M. *Jeremiah: Pain and Promise*. Minneapolis, MN: Fortress Press, 2012.

Peterson, Eugene. *Run with the Horses: The Quest for Life at Its Best*. Downers Grove, IL: InterVarsity Press, 2019.

Sandberg, Sheryl. *Option B: Facing Adversity, Building Resilience, and Finding Joy*. New York, NY: Knopf, 2017.

Shead, Andrew G. *A Mouth Full of Fire: The Word of God in the Words of Jeremiah*. New Studies in Biblical Theology, Vol. 29. Downers Grove, IL: InterVarsity Press, 2012.

Wright, N. T. *Surprised by Hope: Rethinking Heaven, the Resurrection, and the Mission of the Church*. San Francisco, CA: HarperOne, 2008.

NOTES

Chapter 1: Invitation to Hope

1. George Herring, *An Introduction to the History of the Church* (New York: Continuum International Publishing Group, 2006), 320.

2. Lindsey Crouse, "Why I Stopped Running During the Pandemic (And How I Started Again)," *The New York Times*, March 7, 2021, https://www.nytimes.com/2021/03/07/opinion/pandemic-wall-fitness-running.html.

3. "The State of Mental Health in America," *Mental Health America*, https://www.mhanational.org/issues/state-mental-health-america.

4. "New APA Poll Shows Surge in Anxiety Among Americans Top Causes Are Safety, COVID-19, Health, Gun Violence, and the Upcoming Election," *American Psychological Association*, October 21, 2020, https://www.psychiatry.org/newsroom/news-releases/anxiety-poll-2020.

5. Eugene Peterson, *A Long Obedience in the Same Direction* (Downers Grove, IL: InterVarsity Press, 2000).

6. We recognize that the stories in this book are told with the benefit of hindsight. Looking back in retrospect on their journeys grants each leader perspective and clarity we are not always afforded in the midst of pain or struggle. Yet we also trust that our steps and stories are guided by God and marked by His grace. One day we, too, will look back with the gift of hindsight.

7. Matthew 6:10b

8. Bryan Stevenson, *Just Mercy* (New York: Spiegel & Grau, 2014), 289.

9. "Overcoming Pandemic Fatigue: How to Reenergize Organizations for the Long Run," *McKinsey & Company*, November 25, 2020, https://www.mckinsey.com/business-functions/organization/our-insights/overcoming-pandemic-fatigue-how-to-reenergize-organizations-for-the-long-run.

10. Jay Dixit, "George Carlin's Last Interview," *Psychology Today*, June 23, 2008, https://www.psychologytoday.com/us/blog/brainstorm/200806/george-carlins-last-interview.

11. I (Peter) heard this analogy of the balcony and dance floor by Ron Heifitz at Harvard Kennedy School, 2003.

12. Andrew Byers, "Is Christian Cynicism a Spiritual Sickness?" *Christianity Today*, May 30, 2011, https://www.christianitytoday.com/biblestudies/articles/spiritualformation /faithwithoutillusions.html.

13. Kenneth Walsh, "A Nation of Cynics," *U.S. News*, January 5, 2018, https://www .usnews.com/news/the-report/articles/2018-01-05/president-trump-is-leading-a-nation -of-cynics.

14. Mohammed Fairouz, "The Age of Cynicism," On Being, July 25, 2015, https:// onbeing.org/blog/the-age-of-cynicism.

15. Jeremiah 17:8 MSG

16. Hebrews 10:23

Chapter 2: False Hope

1. Anne Frank, *Anne Frank's Tales from the Secret Annex: A Collection of Her Short Stories, Fables, and Lesser-Known Writings* (New York: Bantam Publishing, 2003 Reprint Edition), 121.

2. *Annie*, directed by Will Gluck (Culver City, CA: Columbia Pictures, 2014).

3. Timothy Keller, "Hope for the World," *Gospel in Life*, September 27, 2009, https://gospelinlife.com/downloads/hope-for-the-world-6022/.

4. Eugene Peterson, *Run with the Horses: The Quest for Life at Its Best* (Downers Grove, IL: InterVarsity Press, 2019), 23.

Chapter 3: Faint Hope

1. John Mark Comer, "Cultivating Hope with John Mark Comer," *Reality San Francisco Podcast*, April 30, 2020.

2. Even Jesus, who knew that the untimely death of his friend Lazarus was not the end of the story, wept.

3. Soong-Chan Rah, *Prophetic Lament* (Downers Grove, IL: InterVarsity Press, 2015), 68.

4. Habakkuk 3:17–19

5. Habakkuk 3:19

6. Daniel Goleman, *Social Intelligence* (New York: Bantam, 2006), 54.

7. Tawnell Hobbs and Lee Hawkins, "The Results Are In for Remote Learning: It Didn't Work," *The Wall Street Journal*, June 5, 2020, https://www.wsj.com/articles /schools-coronavirus-remote-learning-lockdown-tech-11591375078.

8. Barbara Brown Taylor, *Gospel Medicine* (Lanham, MD: Cowley Publications, 1995), 74.

9. Name changed to protect his identity.

Chapter 4: Forgotten Hope

1. N. T. Wright, *The Challenge of Jesus* (Downers Grove, IL: InterVarsity Press, 2015), 184.

2. "General Superintendent Emerita Jo Anne Lyon," *The Wesleyan Church*, https:// www.wesleyan.org/gso/jo-anne-lyon.

3. Ibid.

4. "General Superintendent Emerita Jo Anne Lyon," *The Wesleyan Church*, https://www.wesleyan.org/gso/jo-anne-lyon.

5. Ibid.

6. Ibid.

7. Ibid.

8. 1 John 3:17

9. Jeremiah 14:22b ESV

10. Isaiah 40:31a NIV

11. Andy Crouch, *Playing God: Redeeming the Gift of Power* (Downers Grove, IL: InterVarsity Press, 2013), 217.

12. Luke 1:37 ESV

13. Luke 1:38 NIV

14. "About Us," *World Hope International*, https://www.worldhope.org/about-us.

15. Jo Anne Lyon, "Leading Well in Times of Crisis," *National Association of Evangelicals*, May 15, 2020, https://www.nae.net/lyonpodcast/.

Chapter 5: Upward

1. Timothy Keller, *Counterfeit Gods: The Empty Promises of Money, Sex, and Power, and the Only Hope That Matters* (London: Penguin Books, 2011), 154.

2. Jeremiah 10:8a

3. Jeremiah 17:5–6 MSG

4. Jeremiah 17:7–8

5. John 15:4b, 5b

6. Kyle Idleman, *Don't Give Up* (Grand Rapids: Baker Books, 2019), 43.

7. Anne Helen Peterson, *Can't Even: How Millennials Became the Burnout Generation* (Boston: HMH Books, 2020), xxix.

8. Psalm 121:1–2

9. Hebrews 12:1b–2a

Chapter 6: An Unexpected Guide

1. Jeremiah 1:10

2. Walter Brueggemann, *Hopeful Imagination: Prophetic Voices in Exile* (Philadelphia, PA: Fortress Press, 1986), 29.

3. Samuel Hildebrandt, personal communication with authors, February 26, 2021. "There are scenes of verbal attacks (11:19, 21; 15:10; 17:15; 18:18; 20:10; 26:7–9) but also much physical abuse in the form of beatings (20:2), imprisonment (32:3), the despair of the hopeless pit (38:6), and a forceful abduction (43:5–6)." This maltreatment comes even from religious leaders (20:1–2) and political leaders (38:1–6) from Jeremiah's hometown of Anathoth (11:21–23).

4. "An Overview of the Book of Jeremiah," *Theology of Work Project*, https://www.theologyofwork.org/old-testament/jeremiah-lamentations/an-overview-of-the-book-of-jeremiah.

5. *ESV Study Bible* (Wheaton, IL: Crossway Bibles, 2007).

6. Jeremiah 20:7a

7. Samuel Hildebrandt, personal communication with the authors, February 26, 2021. "No other prophet, not even Moses, levels such harsh accusations against God as Jeremiah in 4:10; 12:1–4; 15:18; 20:7 . . . to the point that he'll prefer not to play a part at all in God's work and world (20:14–18)."

8. Jeremiah 1:19a

9. Jeremiah 2:11, 18

10. Jeremiah 2:13

11. Kathleen O'Connor. *Jeremiah: Pain and Promise* (Minneapolis: Fortress Press, 2012), 37.

12. Jeremiah 2:34

13. Jeremiah 1:9

14. Jeremiah 2:9

15. Jeremiah 7:1–10; Brueggemann, *Hopeful Imagination*, 19.

16. Jeremiah 38

17. Brueggemann, *Hopeful Imagination*, 22.

18. Samuel Hildebrandt, personal communication with the authors, February 26, 2021. "There are many instances of hope in Jeremiah, e.g., the promise of 'building and planting' (1:10), the vision of renewal in 3:14–18, the assurance that judgment will not be a 'full end' (4:27; 5:10; 18), God's world-wide rule (10:1–16), a new exodus (16:14–21), new leaders in the future (23:1–8). Hope is scattered amidst judgment all the way through the first half and continues in chapters 26–52 (e.g., Ebed-Melech saving Jeremiah from the cistern in chapter 38 or the death of the corrupt king in chapter 39). There are seeds of hope all through the book: death and life, disillusion, and new vision are often two sides of the same coin in Jeremiah. Again, 1:10 is the program for the entire book."

19. Genesis 3:3–7

20. Genesis 3:23–24

21. 1 Peter 1:1

22. 2 Kings 18:9–12 (Assyrians); 2 Kings 24:10–16 (Babylonians); Luke 2 (Romans)

23. Matthew 6:10b

24. Jeremiah 17:7–8

25. This message resembles the words God spoke to His people in Deuteronomy 8:17–18: "You may say to yourself, 'My power and the strength of my hands have produced this wealth for me.' But remember the LORD your God, for it is he who gives you the ability to produce wealth, and so confirms his covenant, which he swore to your ancestors, as it is today" (NIV).

26. Jeremiah 2:13; 17:13

27. Jeremiah 10:15–16a

28. Jeremiah 29:7a

29. Jeremiah 14:22

Chapter 7: Enduring Hope

1. Eugene Peterson, *Run with the Horses*, 172.

2. Amos 5:24 ESV

3. Via Samuel Hildebrandt in personal communication with the authors, February 26, 2021. "Jeremiah 29:11 ranked number one among user searches on BibleGateway.com in 2018 (https://www.biblegateway.com/year-in-review/2018/ [accessed 31

March 2020]) and number one of the verses users of YouVersion 'shared, bookmarked, and highlighted most often in 2018' in Australia, Canada, Ghana, Japan, Nigeria, the United Kingdom, and other countries" (https://docs.google.com/spreadsheets /d/1jX3RkR62wlwcIR-yA-F1grN84x8DgFhwbfpyQj1qWz0/edit#gid=0 [accessed 31 March 2020]).

4. Samuel Hildebrandt, personal communication with the authors, February 26, 2021, citing Jeremiah 24:1 and 29:2.

5. Samantha Power, "How to Kill a Country," *The Atlantic*, December 2003, https:// www.theatlantic.com/magazine/archive/2003/12/how-to-kill-a-country/302845.

6. Steve Hanke, "Zimbabwe's Hyperinflation: The Correct Number is 89 Sextillion Percent," *CATO Institute*, June 3, 2016, https://www.cato.org/blog/zimbabwes -hyperinflation-correct-number-89-sextillion-percent.

7. Jeremiah 8:21

8. "Zimbabwe Anglicans to Return to Churches After Supreme Court Ruling," *Episcopal News Service*, November 19, 2012, https://www.episcopalnewsservice.org /2012/11/19/zimbabwe-anglicans-to-return-to-churches-after-supreme-court-ruling/.

9. Philippians 1:20

10. Samuel Hildebrandt, personal communication with the authors, February 26, 2021.

11. Kathleen O'Connor, *Jeremiah: Pain and Promise* (Minneapolis: Fortress Press, 2012), 19.

12. Jeremiah 17:5

13. Brueggemann, *Hopeful Imagination*, 4.

14. Ezekiel 37:11

15. Ezekiel 37:5–6

16. Brueggemann, *Hopeful Imagination*, 83.

Chapter 8: Suffering

1. Timothy Keller, *Walking with God Through Pain and Suffering* (London: Penguin Books, 2015), 5.

2. José Corpas, "In the Valley of Lemons," *Plough*, February 1, 2020, https://www .plough.com/en/topics/justice/social-justice/in-the-valley-of-lemons.

3. "About Us," Lemonade International, https://www.lemonadeinternational.org /about/la-limonada/.

4. José Alejandro Adamuz Hortelano, "El barranco de las pandillas [The gangs' ravine]," *El País*, September 30, 2015, https://elpais.com/elpais/2015/09/29/planeta_fu turo/1443525680_735932.html.

5. Ibid.

6. Jeremiah 12:1–3

7. Jeremiah 12:5

8. Jeremiah 11:21–23

9. David Melvin, "Why does the way of the wicked prosper? Human and divine suffering in Jeremiah 11:18–12:23 and the problem of evil," *Andrews University*, https://www.andrews.edu/weblmsc/moodle/public/courses/relb274/lesson08/L9%20D %20Melvin%20Human%20and%20Divine%20Suffering%20in%20Jeremiah.pdf.

10. Jeremiah 12:7

11. Eugene Peterson, *Run with the Horses*, 169.

12. David Melvin, "Why does the way of the wicked prosper? Human and divine suffering in Jeremiah 11:18–12:23 and the problem of evil," *Andrews University*, https://www.andrews.edu/weblmsc/moodle/public/courses/relb274/lesson08/L9%20D%20Melvin%20Human%20and%20Divine%20Suffering%20in%20Jeremiah.pdf.

13. José Alejandro Adamuz Hortelano, "El barranco de las pandillas [The gangs' ravine]," *El País*, September 30, 2015, https://elpais.com/elpais/2015/09/29/planeta_futuro/1443525680_735932.html.

14. *Lemonade International*, https://www.lemonadeinternational.org/.

15. John 16:33b NIV

16. John 16:2

17. John 16:33

18. Ryan Nelson, "How Did the Apostles Die? What We Actually Know," *OverviewBible*, December 17, 2019, https://overviewbible.com/how-did-the-apostles-die/.

19. Philippians 2:8

20. John 16:33b

21. C. S. Lewis, *The Problem of Pain* (New York: HarperCollins, 2001), 91.

22. Charles H. Spurgeon, *Spurgeon's Sermons on Great Prayers of the Bible* (Grand Rapids, MI: Kregel Academic, 1996), 31.

23. Uri Friedman, "David Brooks's 5-Step Guide to Being Deep," *The Atlantic*, July 1, 2014, theatlantic.com/national/archive/2014/07/david-brooks-5-step-guide-to-being-deep/373699/.

24. Jeremiah 17:8

25. John 16:33b

26. John 16:33 NKJV

27. Ephesians 1:18–20

28. John Macmurray, "Chapter Eight: Reflection and the Future," *The Gifford Lectures*, https://www.giffordlectures.org/books/persons-relation/chapter-eight-reflection-and-future.

29. 1 Peter 5:10

Chapter 9: Surrender

1. Beth Moore, *Breaking Free* (Nashville: B&H Publishing, 2007), 6.

2. "Palestinian refugees and the right to return," *American Friends Service Committee*, afsc.org/resource/palestinian-refugees-and-right-return.

3. John 1:1 NIV

4. Later that week, Tass opened up to his son, Benali, about his radical conversion. Benali, who was eighteen at the time, threw his arms around his dad. He had secretly given his life to Christ three months prior, but out of fear of his father throwing him out of the house (or worse), he kept quiet about it. After seeking guidance from his church pastor, Benali had returned home, determined to love his father even more. The pastor had set up a 24/7 prayer chain for the family three months before Tass's conversion.

5. "Who We Are," *Hope for Ishmael*, https://www.hopeforishmael.org/who-we-are.html.

6. Jeremiah 1:8

7. Jeremiah 18:4

Chapter 10: Commitment

1. Eugene Peterson, *Run with the Horses*, 159.
2. Similar story to "The Story Behind 'He Ain't Heavy,'" *Boys Town*, June 9, 2017, https://www.boystown.org/blog/Pages/story-behind-aint-heavy.aspx.
3. Jeremiah 1:5
4. Jeremiah 1:6
5. Samuel Hildebrandt, personal communication with the authors, February 26, 2021. "Though Jeremiah's age and lack of experience are in view in the response to his call, it likely has more to do with his low social standing: 'He is young and without a commanding presence and authority,' wrote William McKane," *A Critical and Exegetical Commentary on Jeremiah*, Vol. I. Introduction and Commentary on Jeremiah I–XXV (ICC; Edinburgh: T&T Clark, 1986), 7. "He wouldn't get a hearing in the authority structures of the day."
6. Eugene Peterson, *Run with the Horses*, 48.
7. Jeremiah 1:7–8
8. 2 Corinthians 12:9

Chapter 11: Outward

1. Brueggemann, *Hopeful Imagination*, 33.
2. Genesis 12:2b, 3b ESV, emphasis added
3. Leviticus 19:33–34
4. Joshua W. Jipp, *Saved by Faith and Hospitality* (Grand Rapids: Eerdmans Publishing, 2017), 139.
5. "Exodus 13:3 Cross References," *Open Bible*, https://www.openbible.info/labs /cross-references/search?q=Exodus+13%3A3.
6. Deuteronomy 24:17–18
7. Like us, God's people failed to fully embody what He had called them to be. Yet, in His great mercy and grace, God did not abandon them; He continued to invite them to partner with Him in His redemptive work, just as He does today.
8. "Quotes by Paulo Freire," The Paulo Freire Institute, https://www.freire.org/paulo -freire/quotes-by-paulo-freire.
9. Jeremiah 1:10; 25; 46–51
10. Jeremiah 2:34
11. Jeremiah 22:3
12. Jeremiah 22:15b
13. Jeremiah 22:16
14. Jeremiah 22:17
15. Jeremiah 29:5–7
16. Matthew 5:43–45a
17. 1 Thessalonians 1:3 NIV

Chapter 12: Justice

1. Chris Brewster, Twitter post, December 1, 2020, 4:53 p.m., https://twitter.com /CbrewsterOKC/status/1333892028569096203.

2. Arne Duncan, "Education: The 'Great Equalizer,'" *Britannica*, March 19, 2021, https://www.britannica.com/topic/Education-The-Great-Equalizer-2119678.

3. Cameron Brenchley, "In America, Education is Still the Great Equalizer," *Homeroom: The Official Blog of the U.S. Department of Education*, December 12, 2011, https://blog.ed.gov/2011/12/in-america-education-is-still-the-great-equalizer/.

4. David Rhode, Kristina Cooke, and Himanshu-Ojha, "The Decline of the 'Great Equalizer,'" *The Atlantic*, December 19, 2012, https://www.theatlantic.com/business/archive/2012/12/the-decline-of-the-great-equalizer/266455/.

5. Michael Leachman and Eric Figueroa, "K-12 School Funding Up in Most 2018 Teacher-Protest States, But Still Well Below Decade Ago," *Center on Budget and Policy Priorities*, March 6, 2019, https://www.cbpp.org/research/state-budget-and-tax/k-12-school-funding-up-in-most-2018-teacher-protest-states-but-still#:~:text=On%20average%2C%2047%20percent%20of,comes%20from%20the%20federal%20government.

6. Sarah Mervosh, "How Much Wealthier Are White School Districts Than Nonwhite Ones? $23 Billion, Report Says," *The New York Times*, February 27, 2019, https://www.nytimes.com/2019/02/27/education/school-districts-funding-white-minorities.html.

7. Inga Saffron, "Philly didn't become America's poorest city by chance. Here's how we fix it," *The Philadelphia Inquirer*, October 13, 2020, https://www.inquirer.com/business/philadelphia-poverty-unemployment-racism-education-upskilling-20201013.html.

8. Jill Barshay, "Rich schools get richer," *The Hechinger Report*, June 8, 2020, https://hechingerreport.org/rich-schools-get-richer.

9. David Rhode, Kristina Cooke, and Himanshu-Ojha, "The Decline of the 'Great Equalizer'," *The Atlantic*, December 19, 2012, https://www.theatlantic.com/business/archive/2012/12/the-decline-of-the-great-equalizer/266455/.

10. Ray Carter, "As public charter schools come under attack, parents, school officials tout success," *Oklahoma Council of Public Affairs*, June 6, 2019, https://www.ocpathink.org/post/as-public-charter-schools-come-under-attack-parents-school-officials-tout-success?print.

11. Next Thought, "The Power of Connections: Interview with Chris Brewster, Superintendent of Santa Fe South Schools in Oklahoma City," *Vimeo*, https://vimeo.com/130366732.

12. Ibid.

13. "Educational Opportunities in the U.S.," *The Educational Opportunity Project at Stanford University*, https://edopportunity.org/explorer/#/map/us/districts/avg/ses/all/9.13/35.58/-97.37/4226010,40.86,-77.14+4222140,41.21,-77.04+1703420,41.05,-88.65+4025230,34.99,-97.39+4032280,35.69,-97.06+4022770,35.47,-97.53.

14. Genesis 18:18

15. For examples, see Deuteronomy 15:1–15 and Leviticus 25:10.

16. Deuteronomy 10:17–19

17. Jeremiah 7:5–7

18. John M. Bracke, "Justice in the Book of Jeremiah," *Word and World* from Luther Seminary, 2002, https://wordandworld.luthersem.edu/content/pdfs/22-4_Jeremiah/22-4_Bracke.pdf.

19. Ibid.

20. See Jeremiah 21:11–14; 22:1–5; 22:13–19; and 23:5–6.

21. Jeremiah 22:3

22. Elliot Dorff and Danya Ruttenberg, eds., *Jewish Choices, Jewish Voices: Social Justice, Volume 6* (Philadelphia, PA: The Jewish Publication Society, 2010), 142.

23. Rev. Dr. Patrick T. O'Neill, "And how are the children?" sermon, First Parish Framingham, MA, https://www.leadrighttoday.com/uploads/9/4/1/6/9416169/andhow arethechildrenessaypermissiongranted.pdf.

24. Ray Carter, "As public charter schools come under attack, parents, school officials tout success," *Oklahoma Council of Public Affairs*, June 6, 2019, https://www .ocpathink.org/post/as-public-charter-schools-come-under-attack-parents-school -officials-tout-success?print.

25. The Oklahoman Editorial Board, "Oklahoma charter schools celebrate 20 years," *The Oklahoman*, October 13, 2013, https://oklahoman.com/article/5643807 /oklahoma-charter-schools-celebrate-20-years.

26. Chris Brewster, Twitter post, November 23, 2020, 1:31 p.m., https://twitter.com /CbrewsterOKC/status/1330942026632876032.

27. Chris Brewster, Twitter post, November 30, 2020, 3:34 p.m., https://twitter.com /CbrewsterOKC/status/1333509766304444418.

28. "Santa Fe South HS," *Oklahoma School Report Cards*, https://oklaschools.com /school/2005/.

29. Brett Dickerson, "Charter school leader in OKC criticizes state A-F school report card system," *Oklahoma City Free Press*, December 6, 2009, https://freepressokc.com /charter-school-leader-in-okc-criticizes-state-a-f-school-report-card-system/.

30. "Educational Opportunities in Oklahoma," *The Educational Opportunity Project at Stanford University*, https://edopportunity.org/explorer/#/map/ok/schools/avg /frl/all/15.5/35.42/-97.51/402277002386,35.42,-97.51.

31. *The Educational Opportunity Project at Stanford University*, https://edoppor tunity.org/.

32. "Educator Profile," *Milken Educator Awards*, https://www.milkeneduca- torawards.org/educators/view/chris-brewster.

33. Next Thought, "The Power of Connections: Interview with Chris Brewster, Superintendent of Santa Fe South Schools in Oklahoma City," *Vimeo*, https://vimeo .com/130366732.

Chapter 13: Sacrifice

1. Throughout this chapter, names have been changed for security.

2. Jeremiah 2:25

3. Matthew Henry, "Commentary on Jeremiah 2," *Blue Letter Bible*, https://www .blueletterbible.org/Comm/mhc/Jer/Jer_002.cfm.

4. Jeremiah 2:2

5. Jeremiah 2:8 ESV

6. Jeremiah 2:11b

7. Matthew 6:24

8. Matthew 16:26a ESV

9. Matthew 19:16–22

10. "Global Estimates of Modern Slavery," *International Labour Office*, 2017, https://www.ilo.org/wcmsp5/groups/public/@dgreports/@dcomm/documents/publi cation/wcms_575479.pdf.

Chapter 14: Forgiveness

1. Corrie ten Boom, *Clippings from My Notebook* (Nashville, TN: Thomas Nelson, Inc., 1982), 19.

2. Alicia Lee and Paul P. Murphy, "A grandmother played 'Auld Lang Syne' on a piano surrounded by rubble from the Beirut explosion," *CNN*, August 5, 2020, https://www.cnn.com/2020/08/05/middleeast/beirut-explosion-auld-lang-syne-piano-trnd /index.html.

3. "Syrian Troops Leave Lebanon After 29-Year Occupation," *The New York Times*, April 26, 2005, https://www.nytimes.com/2005/04/26/international/middleeast/syrian -troops-leave-lebanon-after-29year-occupation.html.

4. Mordechai Nisan, "The Syrian Occupation of Lebanon," *Ariel Center for Policy Research (ACPR)*, http://www.acpr.org.il/publications/books/syria-4-in-1-nisan.pdf.

5. Ibid.

6. "Lebanon 2017 International Religious Freedom Report," *United States Department of State*, 2017, https://web.archive.org/web/20180529205709/https://www.state .gov/documents/organization/281238.pdf.

7. "Background: Facts and figures about 2006 Israel-Hezbollah war," *United Nations Office for the Coordination of Humanitarian Affairs*, July 12, 2007, https://reliefweb .int/report/lebanon/background-facts-and-figures-about-2006-israel-hezbollah-war.

8. "FACTBOX: Costs of war and recovery in Lebanon and Israel," *Reuters*, July 9, 2007, https://www.reuters.com/article/us-lebanon-war-cost/factbox-costs-of-war-and -recovery-in-lebanon-and-israel-idUSL0822571220070709.

9. John 9:3

10. "Lebanon Events of 2008," *Human Rights Watch*, https://www.hrw.org/world -report/2009/country-chapters/lebanon.

11. "Syrian Refugee Crisis Explained," *USA for UNHCR*, https://www.unrefugees .org/news/syria-refugee-crisis-explained/.

12. Dickens Thunde, interview with Peter Greer, July 24, 2020.

13. "Weekly Sermon Illustration: Anger," *The Frederick Buechner Center*, August 26, 2016, https://www.frederickbuechner.com/blog/2016/8/26/weekly-sermon-illustration -anger.

14. Jeremiah 31:34b

15. Jeremiah 50:20

16. Lamentations 3:22–23

17. Matthew 5:44–45a

18. Jeremiah 5:1 MSG

19. Luke 23:34a

20. Matthew 6:12

21. 2 Corinthians 5:20

22. "Lebanon Events of 2018," *Human Rights Watch*, https://www.hrw.org/world -report/2019/country-chapters/lebanon.

Chapter 15: Onward

1. 1 Corinthians 15:58 ESV
2. 2 Corinthians 4:17 NIV
3. 2 Corinthians 12:7
4. 2 Corinthians 6:4b–5 ESV
5. 2 Corinthians 4:18
6. Lamentations 3:25 ESV
7. Aaron De Smet, Laura Tegelberg, Rob Theunissen, and Tiffany Vogel, "Overcoming pandemic fatigue: How to reenergize organizations for the long run," *McKinsey & Company*, https://www.mckinsey.com/business-functions/organization/our-insights/overcoming-pandemic-fatigue-how-to-reenergize-organizations-for-the-long-run.

Chapter 16: Discernment

1. Oswald Chambers, "Now This Explains It," *My Utmost for His Highest*, https://utmost.org/classic/now-this-explains-it-classic/.
2. "Apartheid," *The History Channel,* October 7, 2010, https://www.history.com/topics/africa/apartheid.
3. Samuel G. Freedman, "Mission Schools Opened World to Africans, but Left an Ambiguous Legacy," *The New York Times*, December 27, 2013, https://www.nytimes.com/2013/12/28/us/mission-schools-ambiguous-legacy-in-south-africa.html.
4. Dion Forster, "The Role of the Church in Reconciliation in South Africa," *Lausanne World Pulse Archives*, https://www.lausanneworldpulse.com/themedarticles-php/1267/04-2010.
5. Lucas Laursen, "How building trust has proved central to overcoming malaria," *Nature Portfolio*, October 17, 2018, https://www.nature.com/articles/d41586-018-06972-3.
6. "Epidemiology of Infectious Diseases: Malaria," *Public Health Action Support Team*, https://www.healthknowledge.org.uk/public-health-textbook/disease-causation-diagnostic/2b-epidemiology-diseases-phs/infectious-diseases/malaria.
7. Bloomberg Philanthropies, "The War on Malaria—Johns Hopkins Malaria Research Institute Scientists Lead the Fight," *YouTube*, https://www.youtube.com/watch?v=WuDnlB6KwFs.
8. "The Reality of Malaria," *United Nations International Children's Emergency Fund*, https://www.unicef.org/media/files/MALARIAFACTSHEETAFRICA.pdf.
9. Henri Nouwen, *Discernment: Reading the Signs of Daily Life* (New York: Harper Collins Publishing, 2015), 5.
10. 1 Samuel 8
11. Jeremiah 22:3a, 5
12. Jeremiah 22:30
13. Ibid. MSG
14. Jeremiah 23:1–3
15. Jeremiah 23:5
16. Jeremiah 31:33b–34a
17. Bloomberg Philanthropies, "The War on Malaria—Johns Hopkins Malaria Research Institute Scientists Lead the Fight," *YouTube*, https://www.youtube.com/watch?v=WuDnlB6KwFs.

18. Phil Thuma, "Can Malaria Really Be Eliminated in Rural Africa?" *J. C. Flowers Foundation*, https://www.jcflowersfoundation.org/uploads/2/4/2/6/24260525/thuma _can_malaria_really_be_eliminated_cbmi_17feb2016.pdf.

19. Jeremiah 17:9

20. Romans 12:2b

21. James 1:5

Chapter 17: Obedience

1. Terry Looper, *Sacred Pace: Four Steps to Hearing God and Aligning Yourself With His Will* (Nashville, TN: Thomas Nelson, 2019), 102.

2. *Central Detroit Christian Community Development*, https://www.centraldetroit christian.org/about/.

3. "On a neighborhood mission: Central Detroit Christian slowly rebuilds houses, commerce in 24-block area of north Detroit," *Crain's Detroit Business*, August 21, 2016, https://www.crainsdetroit.com/article/20160821/NEWS/160829975/central-detroit -christian-slowly-rebuilds-houses-commerce-in-24.

4. Katelyn Beaty, "Faith in a Fallen Empire," *Christianity Today*, January 22, 2013, https://www.christianitytoday.com/ct/2013/january-february/faith-in-fallen-empire .html.

5. Daniel 3:17–18

6. Austin Smith, "'But If Not'—A sermon by Martin Luther King, Jr.," *Blogspot*, https://notoriousbiggins.blogspot.com/2010/01/but-if-not-sermon-by-martin-luther -king.html.

7. Ibid.

8. Florence Muindi, phone interview with Chris Horst, October 19, 2020.

9. Jeremiah 11:4b ESV

10. Jeremiah 17:14–16a

11. Jeremiah 20:9b

12. Alec Hill, "Alec Hill: Inside My Slavery," *Christianity Today*, August 13, 2014, https://www.christianitytoday.com/ct/2014/july-august/alec-hill-inside-my-slavery .html.

13. Jeremiah 10:23

14. Jeremiah 10:10a

15. Jeremiah 20:11a

16. Gretha Boston—Topic, "I'm Gonna Do What the Spirit Says Do," *YouTube*, https://www.youtube.com/watch?v=MDoNyF4q2IQ.

17. Jeremiah 6:10b

18. Jeremiah 7:13 NIV

19. Jeremiah 13:8–10

Chapter 18: Perseverance

1. Attributed to Hudson Taylor.

2. "Inaugural Address of President Marcos," *Republic of the Philippines Official Gazette*, December 30, 1965, https://www.officialgazette.gov.ph/1965/12/30/inaugural -address-of-president-marcos-december-30-1965/.

3. Henry Kamm, "Filipinos Support Marcos Take-Over In Hope of Reform," *The New York Times*, October 30, 1972, https://www.nytimes.com/1972/10/30/archives /filipinos-support-marcos-takeover-in-hope-of-reform-filipinos.html.

4. "Martial Law," *Britannica*, https://www.britannica.com/place/Philippines/Martial -law.

5. Nick Davies, "The $10bn question: what happened to the Marcos millions?" *The Guardian*, May 7, 2016, https://www.theguardian.com/world/2016/may/07/10bn-dollar -question-marcos-millions-nick-davies.

6. Ibid.

7. Jeremiah 20:8b, 7b

8. Jeremiah 20:2

9. Jeremiah 15:18

10. Eugene Peterson, *Run with the Horses*, 88.

11. Jeremiah 40:1

12. Samuel Hildebrandt, personal communication with the authors, February 26, 2021. "We should not overlook just how shocking this symbolic action was—Jeremiah does not simply go and buy the field and rejoice in the hope God has given him. Instead, he questions God's motives in v. 25 [chapter 32]: The Babylonians are at the gates, yet you tell me to buy land? Pamela Scalise is right to speak here of the 'absurdity of God's command,' Gerald L. Keown, Pamela J. Scalise, and Thomas G. Smothers, Jeremiah 26–52 (WBC 27; Dallas, TX: Word Books, 1995), 157. God's signs of hope can, at times, make no sense to us. In Jeremiah 32, God patiently responds in vv. 26–44 to the prophet's query and widens his horizon: Where Jeremiah can see only defeat, God sees the beginning of new life."

13. Jeremiah 32:1–15

14. Jeremiah 32:14 NIV

15. Jeremiah 32:15 NIV

16. Jeremiah 33:8–9a NIV

17. Jeremiah 23:5

18. *Institute for Studies in Asian Church and Culture*, http://isaccnet.weebly.com /development-work.html.

19. Eugene Peterson, *Run with the Horses*, 110.

20. *Institute for Studies in Asian Church and Culture*, http://isaccnet.weebly.com /about-us.html.

21. Jeremiah 23:5–6

Chapter 19: Community

1. Henri Nouwen, "Waiting in Community," *Henri Nouwen Society*, https://henri nouwen.org/meditation/waiting-in-community/.

2. "Country: Poland," Joshua Project: A Ministry of Frontier Ventures, https:// joshuaproject.net/countries/PL.

3. "Young Catholics" refers to those under forty years old.

4. "Young adults around the world are less religious by several measures," Pew Research Center, June 13, 2018, https://www.pewforum.org/2018/06/13/young-adults -around-the-world-are-less-religious-by-several-measures/.

5. "Church attendance in Poland plummeting: report," Radio Poland, May 10, 2018, http://archiwum.thenews.pl/1/11/Artykul/385757,Church-attendance-in-Poland-plummeting-report.

6. "Andrzej Turkanik // Quo Vadis Institute," Praxis, October 16, 2019, https://journal.praxislabs.org/andrzej-turkanik-quo-vadis-institute-df911258624b.

7. Dave Jewitt, personal communication with Peter Greer, December 16, 2020.

8. "Andrzej Turkanik // Quo Vadis Institute," *Praxis*, October 16, 2019, https://journal.praxislabs.org/andrzej-turkanik-quo-vadis-institute-df911258624b.

9. Jeffrey Kranz, "Jeremiah: Jerusalem's rebellion, punishment, and hope," *Overview Bible*, January 16, 2014, https://overviewbible.com/jeremiah/. For more on false prophets, see Jeremiah 5:30–31; 14:13–14; and 23:16.

10. Samuel Hildebrandt, personal correspondence with the authors, February 26, 2021. Jeremiah 11:21–23; 20:1–2; 38:1–6.

11. Jeremiah 36:4

12. Jeremiah 36:5–8

13. Jeremiah 36:19, 26

14. Jeremiah 43:6

15. Jeremiah 26:24

16. Jeremiah 38:7–13

17. The Better Samaritan Podcast, "Undercut the Old Narratives to Show the Love Jesus Requires," Apple Podcasts, https://podcasts.apple.com/us/podcast/the-better-samaritan-podcast/id1544304583?i=1000513032546.

18. "The Loneliness Epidemic," *Health Resources and Services Administration*, https://www.hrsa.gov/enews/past-issues/2019/january-17/loneliness-epidemic.

19. Michael Badriaki, interview with Peter Greer on August 13, 2020.

Conclusion

1. Hebrews 13:7

2. N. T. Wright, *The Crown and the Fire: Meditations on the Cross and the Life of the Spirit* (Grand Rapids, MI: Wm. B. Eerdmans), 80.

3. Matthew 11:28–30 MSG

4. Romans 8:28

5. Madeleine L'Engle, *Walking on Water: Reflections on Faith and Art* (Colorado Springs: Convergent Books, 2016), 22.

6. 1 Corinthians 13:7 NIV

7. Romans 5:5

More from Peter Greer and Chris Horst

Why do so many organizations wander from their mission, while others remain Mission True? Can drift be prevented? In *Mission Drift*, HOPE International executives Peter Greer and Chris Horst show how to determine whether your organization is in danger of drift. You'll discover what you can do to prevent drift or get back on track and how to protect what matters most.

Mission Drift

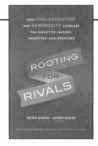

Discover how to expand your ministry by teaming up with so-called *rival* organizations rather than vying for donations. With a countercultural message, a Christlike model, and real-world examples, Greer and Horst reveal the key to revitalizing your ministry, sharing how you can multiply its impact by collaborating rather than competing with others.

Rooting for Rivals

⬧BETHANYHOUSE

 Stay up to date on your favorite books and authors with our free e-newsletters. Sign up today at bethanyhouse.com.

 facebook.com/BHPnonfiction

 @bethany_house

 @bethany_house_nonfiction